JUMBLE® KNOCKOUT

These Puzzles Will Have You Seeing Stars

Henri Arnold
and
Bob Lee

TRIUMPH
BOOKS

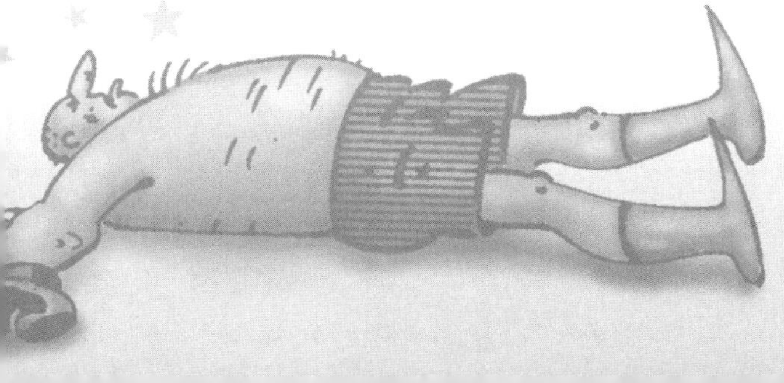

This book is available in quantity at special discounts
for your group or organization.

For further information, contact:

Triumph Books LLC
814 North Franklin Street
Chicago, Illinois 60610
Phone: (312) 337-0747
www.triumphbooks.com

Printed in U.S.A.

ISBN: 978-1-62937-078-1

Design by Sue Knopf

CONTENTS

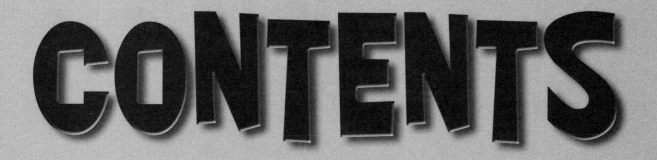

JUMBLE®
KNOCKOUT

Classic Puzzles

PUZZLE 1

JUMBLE®

Unscramble these four Jumbles, one letter to each square, to form four ordinary words.

BAEBY

NARCK

TAUNER

YELMIT

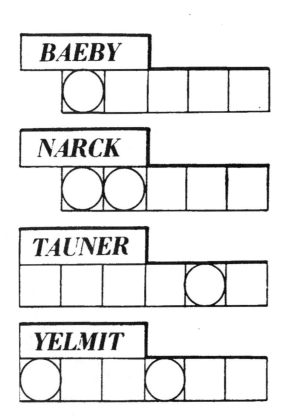

BIGMOUTHED AT THE SUMMIT!

Now arrange the circled letters to form the surprise answer, as suggested by the above cartoon.

Print answer here **A**

PUZZLE 2

JUMBLE®

Unscramble these four Jumbles, one letter to each square, to form four ordinary words.

LEVED

YIFFT

REPTIL

LIDIAN

You check out perfect

WHY THE RESULTS OF HIS PHYSICAL WERE MUSIC TO HIS EARS.

Now arrange the circled letters to form the surprise answer, as suggested by the above cartoon.

Print answer here **HE WAS** ◯◯◯ **AS A** ◯◯◯◯◯◯

PUZZLE 3

JUMBLE®

Unscramble these four Jumbles, one letter to each square, to form four ordinary words.

YOPEN

INARG

KINIBI

RAYVOS

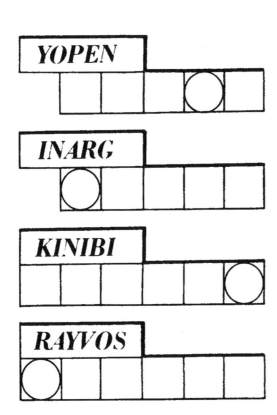

Great to be free . . .
You got a suspended sentence last time
25¢
ONCE IS OK, BUT A REPEAT MEANS PRISON.

Now arrange the circled letters to form the surprise answer, as suggested by the above cartoon.

Print answer here

PUZZLE 4

JUMBLE®

Unscramble these four Jumbles, one letter to each square, to form four ordinary words.

YUMOS

PYLAP

NEEWAK

UMLUTT

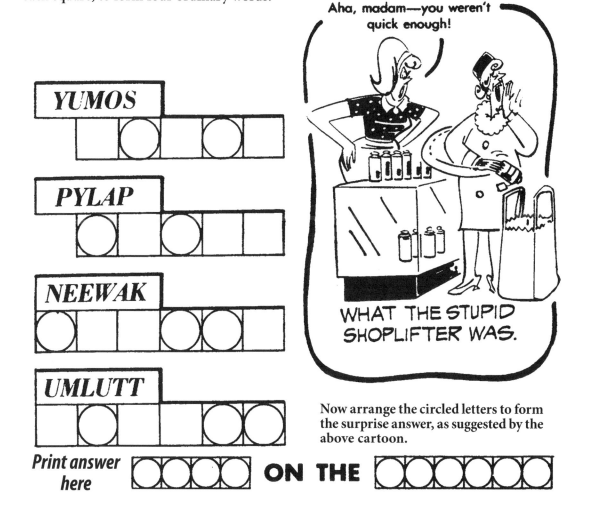

Aha, madam—you weren't quick enough!
WHAT THE STUPID SHOPLIFTER WAS.

Now arrange the circled letters to form the surprise answer, as suggested by the above cartoon.

Print answer here ◯◯◯◯ **ON THE** ◯◯◯◯◯◯

JUMBLE®

Unscramble these four Jumbles, one letter to each square, to form four ordinary words.

TIVER

RIBAN

NESSUC

FALCIE

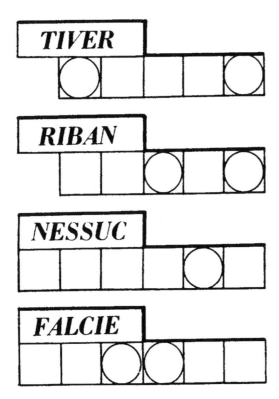

THE CARTOONIST DREW THIS IN ORDER TO HIDE WHAT HE WAS DOING.

Now arrange the circled letters to form the surprise answer, as suggested by the above cartoon.

Print answer here **A**

JUMBLE®

Unscramble these four Jumbles, one letter to each square, to form four ordinary words.

TECOT

DESET

INLOPP

ROVACT

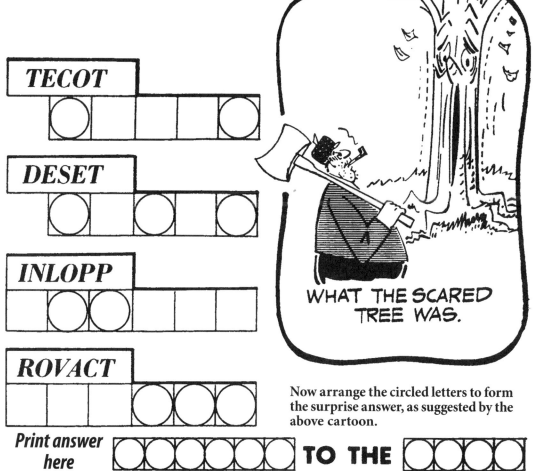

WHAT THE SCARED TREE WAS.

Now arrange the circled letters to form the surprise answer, as suggested by the above cartoon.

Print answer here ______ **TO THE** ____

PUZZLE 7

JUMBLE®

Unscramble these four Jumbles, one letter to each square, to form four ordinary words.

BISSA

NAYRE

CORVEL

UNPOCE

OPENINGS PROVIDED FOR STEREO SOUND.

Now arrange the circled letters to form the surprise answer, as suggested by the above cartoon.

Print answer here

PUZZLE 8

JUMBLE®

Unscramble these four Jumbles, one letter to each square, to form four ordinary words.

PIPNY

TUNDA

GUMSED

DUTOXE

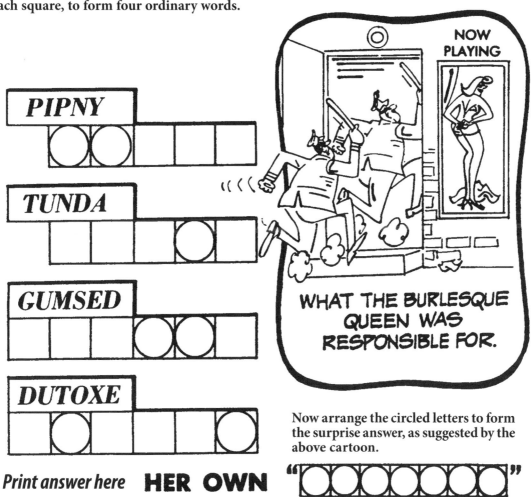

NOW PLAYING
WHAT THE BURLESQUE QUEEN WAS RESPONSIBLE FOR.

Now arrange the circled letters to form the surprise answer, as suggested by the above cartoon.

Print answer here **HER OWN** "___ ___ ___ ___ ___ ___ ___"

PUZZLE 9

JUMBLE®

Unscramble these four Jumbles, one letter to each square, to form four ordinary words.

HUBOG

ETHAL

GURFAL

VERDIN

THIS OLD-FASHIONED GARMENT SOUNDS LIKE TWO.

Now arrange the circled letters to form the surprise answer, as suggested by the above cartoon.

Print answer here **A**

JUMBLE®

Unscramble these four Jumbles, one letter to each square, to form four ordinary words.

SITOC

RIVOS

HALEXE

GROFER

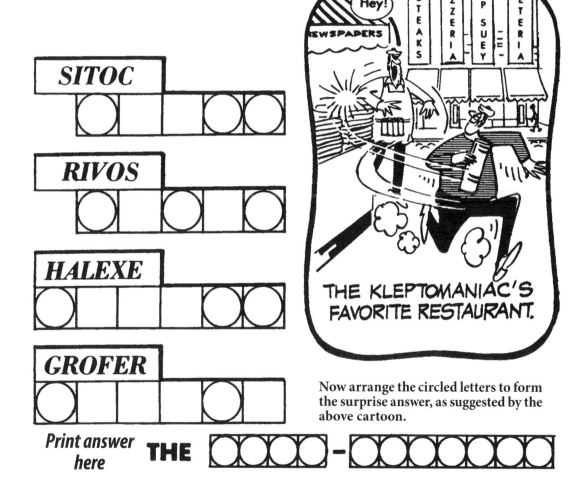

THE KLEPTOMANIAC'S FAVORITE RESTAURANT.

Now arrange the circled letters to form the surprise answer, as suggested by the above cartoon.

Print answer here **THE** ( ) ( ) ( ) ( ) - ( ) ( ) ( ) ( ) ( ) ( ) ( )

PUZZLE 11

JUMBLE®

Unscramble these four Jumbles, one letter to each square, to form four ordinary words.

MOFUR

TAMEL

LORCAR

ENGALB

BEAUTY PARLOR
Look at me!
Look at me!
Yec-c-ch!
WHAT SOME GIRLS DO FOR ATTENTION.

Now arrange the circled letters to form the surprise answer, as suggested by the above cartoon.

Print answer here " ◯◯◯◯◯◯◯ " **FOR IT**

JUMBLE®

Unscramble these four Jumbles, one letter to each square, to form four ordinary words.

Don't need 'em with these shoes
WHEN THE WEATHER IS BAD, ONLY THESE SHOULD TAKE TO THE STREETS.

RINED

SYKAH

RALOPP

WHACES

Now arrange the circled letters to form the surprise answer, as suggested by the above cartoon.

Print answer here

PUZZLE 13

JUMBLE®

Unscramble these four Jumbles, one letter to each square, to form four ordinary words.

GOSUB

RONED

TALKEN

FLEMSY

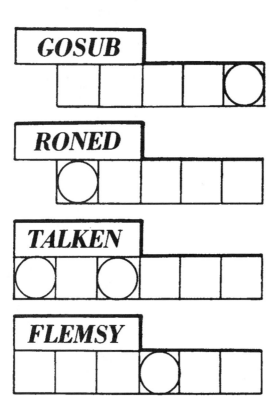

My IQ was higher than all the boys!
Aw, forget it!
WHAT WOMEN WHO KNOW ALL THE ANSWERS NEVER GET.

Now arrange the circled letters to form the surprise answer, as suggested by the above cartoon.

Print answer here

JUMBLE®

Unscramble these four Jumbles, one letter to each square, to form four ordinary words.

FERIG

WETET

SAKMAD

PINELP

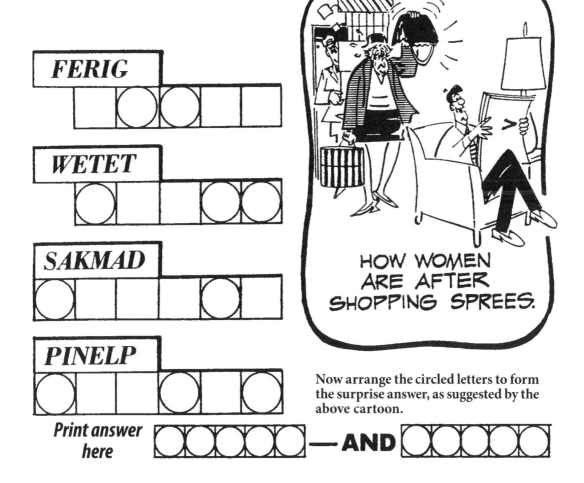

HOW WOMEN ARE AFTER SHOPPING SPREES.

Now arrange the circled letters to form the surprise answer, as suggested by the above cartoon.

Print answer here ◯◯◯◯◯ — **AND** ◯◯◯◯◯

PUZZLE 15

JUMBLE®

Unscramble these four Jumbles, one letter to each square, to form four ordinary words.

PHOWO

NORST

BLABED

WURCEF

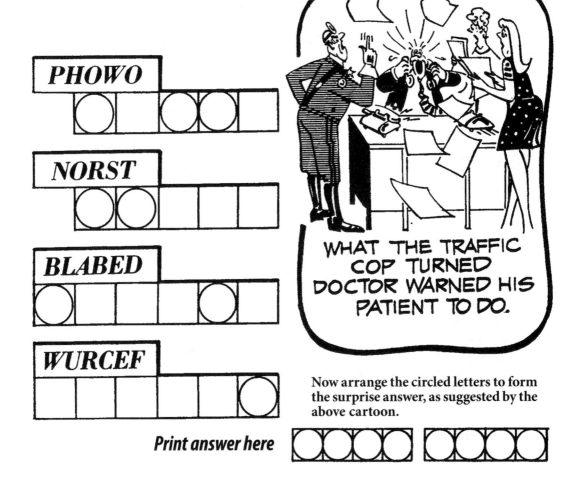

WHAT THE TRAFFIC COP TURNED DOCTOR WARNED HIS PATIENT TO DO.

Now arrange the circled letters to form the surprise answer, as suggested by the above cartoon.

Print answer here

PUZZLE 16

JUMBLE®

Unscramble these four Jumbles, one letter to each square, to form four ordinary words.

DUMON

MAROA

PITTEO

LAFFEB

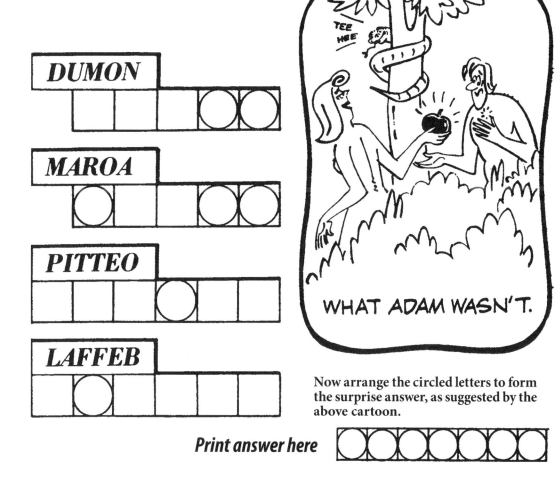

TEE HEE
WHAT ADAM WASN'T.

Now arrange the circled letters to form the surprise answer, as suggested by the above cartoon.

Print answer here

PUZZLE 17

JUMBLE®

Unscramble these four Jumbles, one letter to each square, to form four ordinary words.

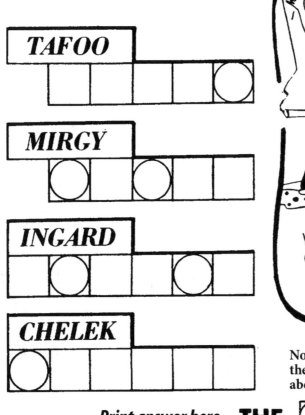

Refill, please
WHAT YOU HAVE TO GET TO WALLPAPER A ROOM.

TAFOO

MIRGY

INGARD

CHELEK

Now arrange the circled letters to form the surprise answer, as suggested by the above cartoon.

Print answer here **THE** ☐☐☐☐ **OF** ☐☐

PUZZLE 18

JUMBLE®

Unscramble these four Jumbles, one letter to each square, to form four ordinary words.

POLEE

BRIHC

NUCHAH

INDAGE

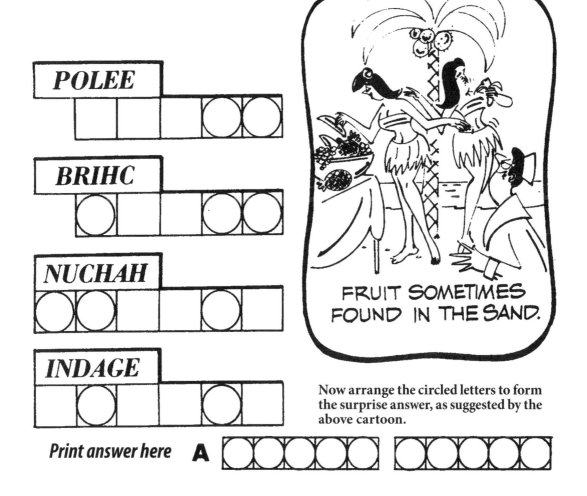

FRUIT SOMETIMES FOUND IN THE SAND.

Now arrange the circled letters to form the surprise answer, as suggested by the above cartoon.

Print answer here **A**

JUMBLE®

Unscramble these four Jumbles, one letter to each square, to form four ordinary words.

KROOB

LAGOW

TIENNY

DEMPIN

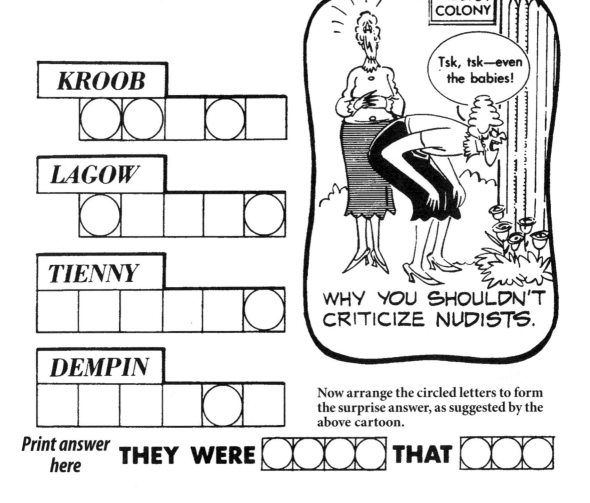

COLONY
Tsk, tsk—even the babies!
WHY YOU SHOULDN'T CRITICIZE NUDISTS.

Now arrange the circled letters to form the surprise answer, as suggested by the above cartoon.

Print answer here **THEY WERE** ◯◯◯◯ **THAT** ◯◯◯

JUMBLE®

Unscramble these four Jumbles, one letter to each square, to form four ordinary words.

IXOCT

SNURP

CEEDDO

ENOMAY

WHAT TO AVOID IF YOU MARRIED YOUR WIFE FOR HER LOOKS.

Now arrange the circled letters to form the surprise answer, as suggested by the above cartoon.

Print answer here

PUZZLE 21

JUMBLE®

Unscramble these four Jumbles, one letter to each square, to form four ordinary words.

PHAMC

DUJEG

BRUMPE

DAGAPO

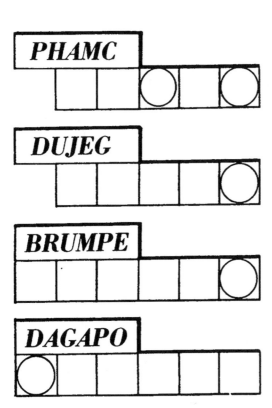

"Groovy, man!
LOVE
WHAT THE HIP GROCER SAID HIS "BAG" WAS.

Now arrange the circled letters to form the surprise answer, as suggested by the above cartoon.

Print answer here

JUMBLE®

Unscramble these four Jumbles, one letter to each square, to form four ordinary words.

ONIGG

EVVAL

YORPOL

HOMFAT

Uh oh! What did you do this time?
YOUR WIFE MIGHT DO THIS WHEN YOU GIVE.

Now arrange the circled letters to form the surprise answer, as suggested by the above cartoon.

Print answer here

JUMBLE®

Unscramble these four Jumbles, one letter to each square, to form four ordinary words.

RIPEV

LOFAR

FRYLUR

PHORTY

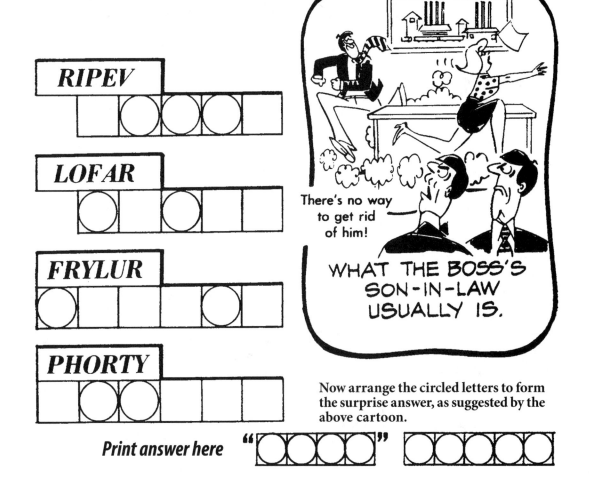

ASBESTOS CO.
There's no way to get rid of him!
WHAT THE BOSS'S SON-IN-LAW USUALLY IS.

Now arrange the circled letters to form the surprise answer, as suggested by the above cartoon.

Print answer here " "

PUZZLE 24

JUMBLE®

Unscramble these four Jumbles, one letter to each square, to form four ordinary words.

RINBY

LAWRC

MILGRY

TRAFYC

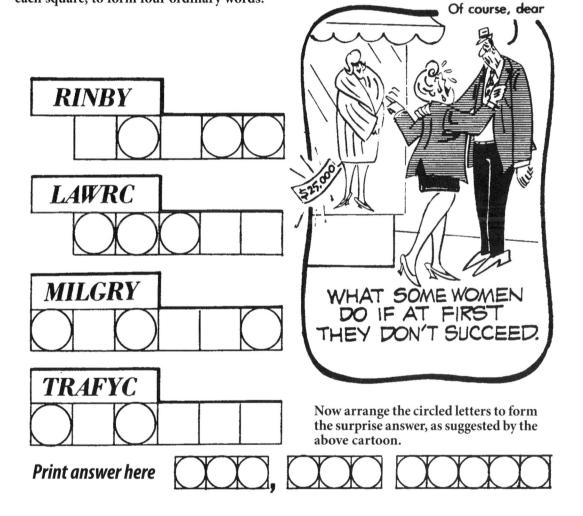

Of course, dear
$25,000
WHAT SOME WOMEN DO IF AT FIRST THEY DON'T SUCCEED.

Now arrange the circled letters to form the surprise answer, as suggested by the above cartoon.

Print answer here ◯◯◯, ◯◯◯ ◯◯◯◯◯

PUZZLE 25

JUMBLE®

Unscramble these four Jumbles, one letter to each square, to form four ordinary words.

GIBLE

DYPET

TALPEA

GALEGH

Thanks for the nickel tip
IT SEEMS ONLY NATURAL THAT "SCOTCH" SHOULD MAKE YOU THIS.

Now arrange the circled letters to form the surprise answer, as suggested by the above cartoon.

Print answer here " "

JUMBLE® KNOCKOUT

Daily Puzzles

PUZZLE 26

JUMBLE®

Unscramble these four Jumbles, one letter to each square, to form four ordinary words.

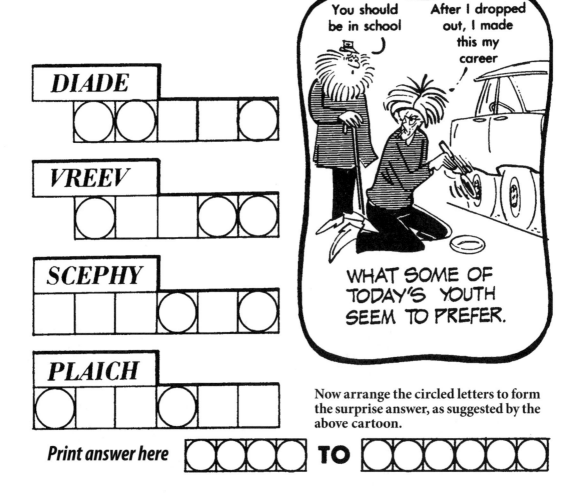

You should be in school
After I dropped out, I made this my career

WHAT SOME OF TODAY'S YOUTH SEEM TO PREFER.

DIADE

VREEV

SCEPHY

PLAICH

Now arrange the circled letters to form the surprise answer, as suggested by the above cartoon.

Print answer here TO

PUZZLE 27

JUMBLE®

Unscramble these four Jumbles, one letter to each square, to form four ordinary words.

SHYKU

EMYTH

VIRFED

SOUNIC

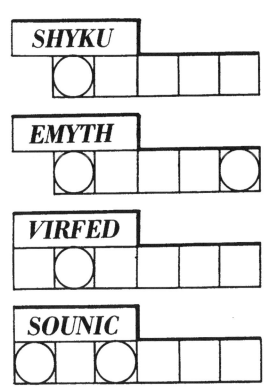

WHAT THE POOLROOM HUSTLER TURNED ACTOR NEVER MISSED.

Now arrange the circled letters to form the surprise answer, as suggested by the above cartoon.

Print answer here

JUMBLE®

Unscramble these four Jumbles, one letter to each square, to form four ordinary words.

YEDEK

RIVOY

SPITTY

YALMIN

Buy anything you like
GOWNS
SOLD
WHEN A BACHELOR GIVES A GIRL PLENTY OF ROPE, THIS IS HOW HE MIGHT FIND HIMSELF.

Now arrange the circled letters to form the surprise answer, as suggested by the above cartoon.

Print answer here ◯◯◯◯ **IN A** ◯◯◯◯◯

JUMBLE®

Unscramble these four Jumbles, one letter to each square, to form four ordinary words.

TAYFF

PINTE

NALIFE

VIRTED

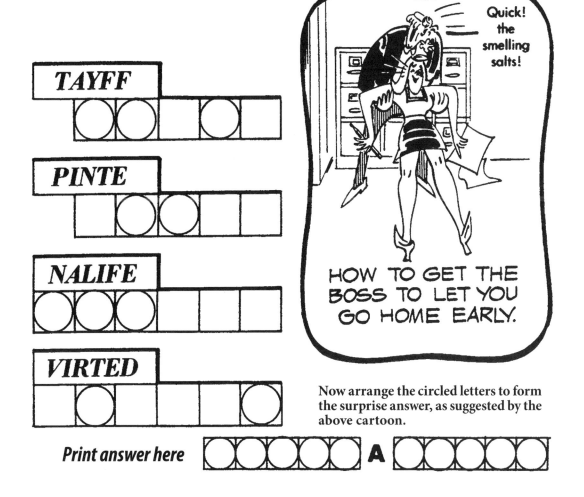

Quick! the smelling salts!
HOW TO GET THE BOSS TO LET YOU GO HOME EARLY.

Now arrange the circled letters to form the surprise answer, as suggested by the above cartoon.

Print answer here ◯◯◯◯◯ A ◯◯◯◯◯

JUMBLE®

Unscramble these four Jumbles, one letter to each square, to form four ordinary words.

CHELE

TYSOO

CRANDI

LARNAC

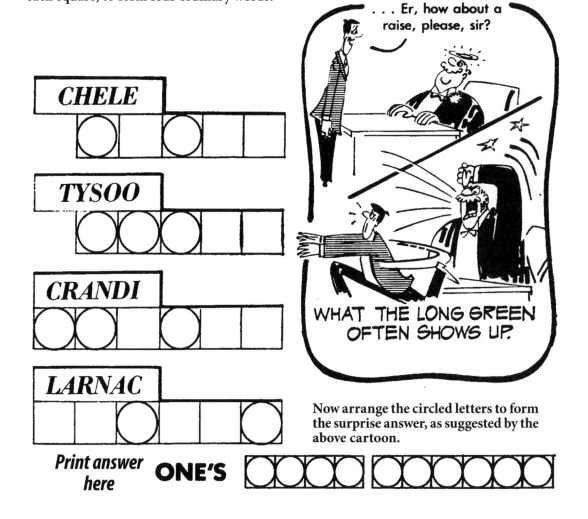

. . . Er, how about a raise, please, sir?
WHAT THE LONG GREEN OFTEN SHOWS UP.

Now arrange the circled letters to form the surprise answer, as suggested by the above cartoon.

Print answer here **ONE'S** ◯◯◯◯ ◯◯◯◯◯◯

JUMBLE®

Unscramble these four Jumbles, one letter to each square, to form four ordinary words.

UPDYM

CHABT

SMALEY

VOINEC

WHAT THE OLD-TIME BREWERS CALLED THEIR ANNUAL SHINDIGS.

Now arrange the circled letters to form the surprise answer, as suggested by the above cartoon.

Print answer here

PUZZLE 32

JUMBLE®

Unscramble these four Jumbles, one letter to each square, to form four ordinary words.

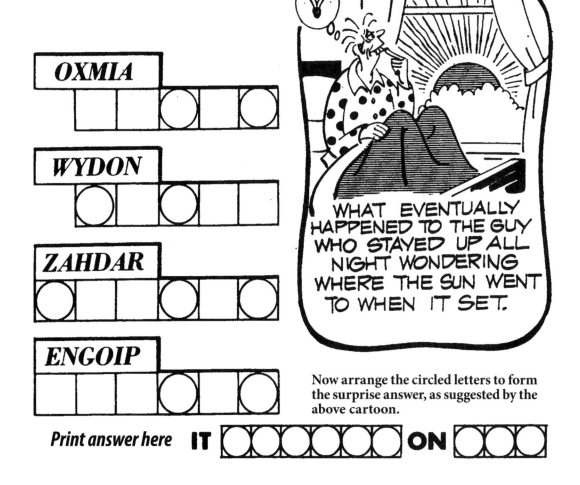

WHAT EVENTUALLY HAPPENED TO THE GUY WHO STAYED UP ALL NIGHT WONDERING WHERE THE SUN WENT TO WHEN IT SET.

OXMIA

☐☐◯☐◯

WYDON

◯☐◯☐☐

ZAHDAR

◯☐☐◯☐◯

ENGOIP

☐☐☐◯☐◯

Now arrange the circled letters to form the surprise answer, as suggested by the above cartoon.

Print answer here **IT** ◯◯◯◯◯◯ **ON** ◯◯◯

PUZZLE **33**

JUMBLE®

Unscramble these four Jumbles, one letter to each square, to form four ordinary words.

MOTEC

DAFEM

CEPTIK

VOGNER

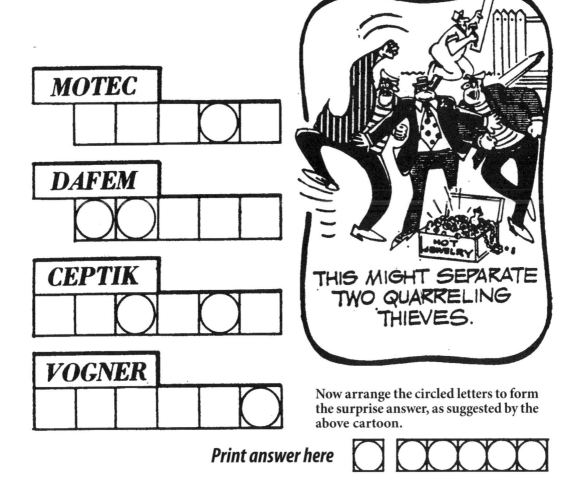

THIS MIGHT SEPARATE TWO QUARRELING THIEVES.

Now arrange the circled letters to form the surprise answer, as suggested by the above cartoon.

Print answer here

PUZZLE 34

JUMBLE®

Unscramble these four Jumbles, one letter to each square, to form four ordinary words.

FAIRE

GITUL

SLABAM

PRETOY

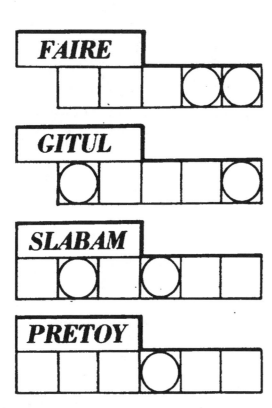

Your drink, sir
Marksman?

WHAT YOU MIGHT AIM FOR IN SOME CIRCLES.

Now arrange the circled letters to form the surprise answer, as suggested by the above cartoon.

Print answer here

JUMBLE®

Unscramble these four Jumbles, one letter to each square, to form four ordinary words.

ALVIA

SEHCS

WHALLO

NORMED

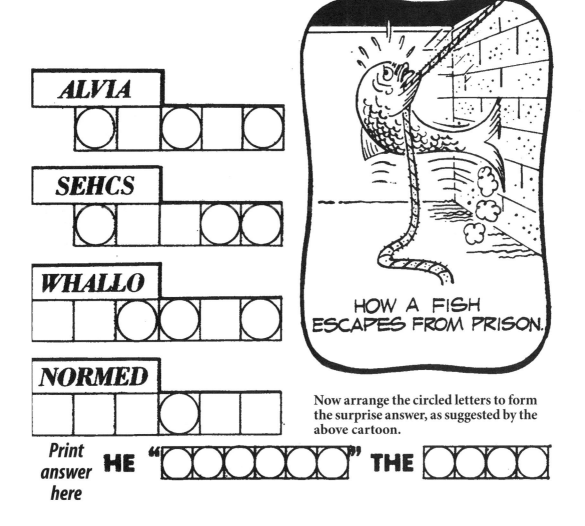

HOW A FISH ESCAPES FROM PRISON.

Now arrange the circled letters to form the surprise answer, as suggested by the above cartoon.

Print answer here HE "◯◯◯◯◯◯" THE ◯◯◯◯

JUMBLE®

Unscramble these four Jumbles, one letter to each square, to form four ordinary words.

ROGAC

MYPTE

UNEAVE

SYMICT

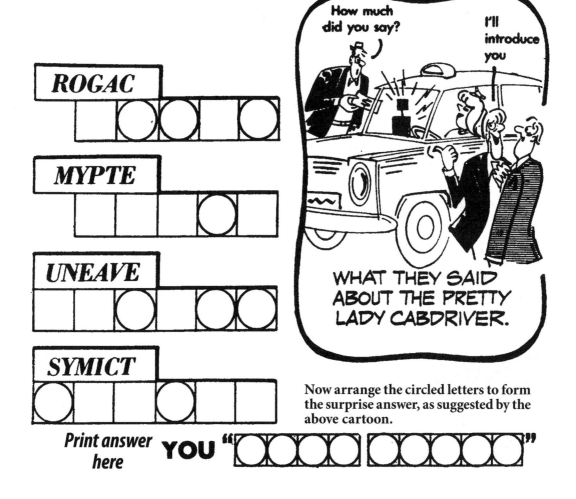

How much did you say?
I'll introduce you
WHAT THEY SAID ABOUT THE PRETTY LADY CABDRIVER.

Now arrange the circled letters to form the surprise answer, as suggested by the above cartoon.

Print answer here **YOU** " "

JUMBLE®

Unscramble these four Jumbles, one letter to each square, to form four ordinary words.

HORAB

UNYTT

PLARIL

ROQUIL

HOW THE DENTIST AND HIS MANICURIST WIFE FOUGHT.

Now arrange the circled letters to form the surprise answer, as suggested by the above cartoon.

Print answer here ○○○○○ & ○○○○

JUMBLE®

Unscramble these four Jumbles, one letter to each square, to form four ordinary words.

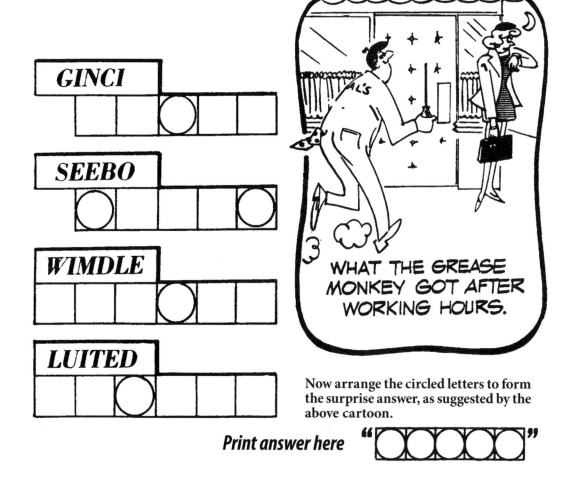

WHAT THE GREASE MONKEY GOT AFTER WORKING HOURS.

GINCI

SEEBO

WIMDLE

LUITED

Now arrange the circled letters to form the surprise answer, as suggested by the above cartoon.

Print answer here " "

PUZZLE 39

JUMBLE®

Unscramble these four Jumbles, one letter to each square, to form four ordinary words.

SAVIT

LUGAH

GLARBE

DORINO

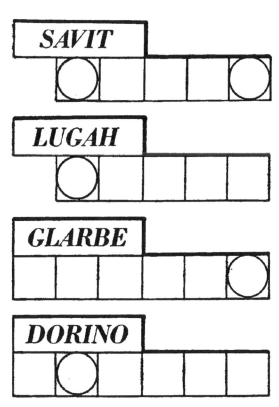

A SMALL DEPRESSION WE ALL HAVE TO STOMACH.

Now arrange the circled letters to form the surprise answer, as suggested by the above cartoon.

Print answer here **THE** ○○○○○

PUZZLE 40

JUMBLE®

Unscramble these four Jumbles, one letter to each square, to form four ordinary words.

GHILT

VERBA

LARFOL

EGMAIP

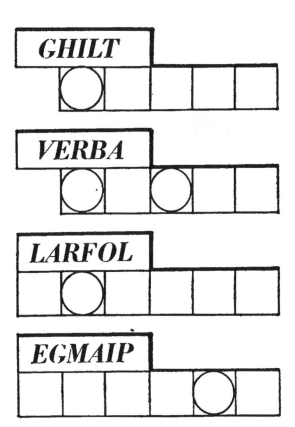

Gilbert
Faraday
Edison
WHIRRRRRR
WHAT AN ELECTRICAL CHARGE MEANS.

Now arrange the circled letters to form the surprise answer, as suggested by the above cartoon.

Print answer here

JUMBLE®

Unscramble these four Jumbles, one letter to each square, to form four ordinary words.

DRECY

NAHVE

TESKUM

ENLOOD

Let's split!
A KIND OF SURREPTITIOUS BALL PLAYING.

Now arrange the circled letters to form the surprise answer, as suggested by the above cartoon.

Print answer here " "

PUZZLE 42

JUMBLE®

Unscramble these four Jumbles, one letter to each square, to form four ordinary words.

LANUN

TAFUL

ABBOMO

GINMOH

WHAT THE BOSS SAID WHEN ASKED HOW MANY PEOPLE WORKED IN HIS OFFICE.

Now arrange the circled letters to form the surprise answer, as suggested by the above cartoon.

Print answer here

PUZZLE 43

JUMBLE®

Unscramble these four Jumbles, one letter to each square, to form four ordinary words.

YILCI

CANKK

DULSHO

AGMANE

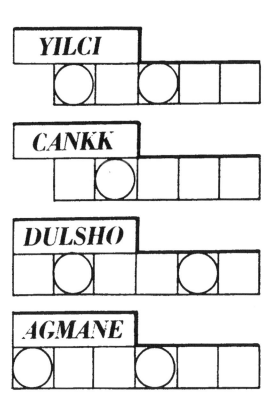

All alone in that big house?
WHAT THE MANICURIST WANTED TO DO.

Now arrange the circled letters to form the surprise answer, as suggested by the above cartoon.

Print answer here

PUZZLE 44

JUMBLE®

Unscramble these four Jumbles, one letter to each square, to form four ordinary words.

DOPKE

VAIST

KLUNIE

CISNEC

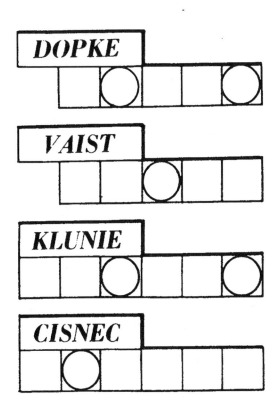

WHAT HE THOUGHT THE RESTAURANT WAS.

Now arrange the circled letters to form the surprise answer, as suggested by the above cartoon.

Print answer here

PUZZLE **45**

JUMBLE®

Unscramble these four Jumbles, one letter to each square, to form four ordinary words.

THAPC

RUFIT

STIGED

CAUPTE

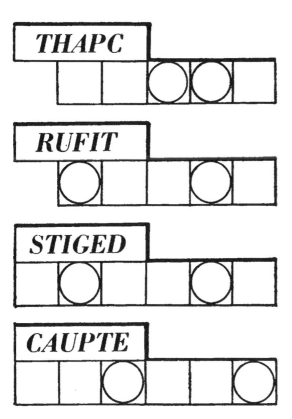

READING: "War and Peace"
A FIGHTING OPPONENT.

Now arrange the circled letters to form the surprise answer, as suggested by the above cartoon.

Print answer here **A**

JUMBLE®

Unscramble these four Jumbles, one letter to each square, to form four ordinary words.

ROARB

PHOCE

HISBUL

MUGLEE

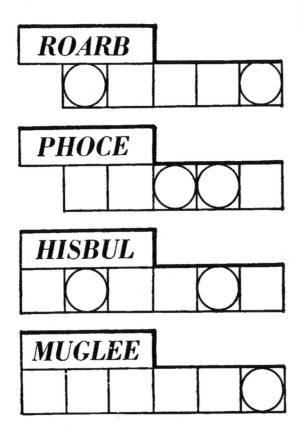

"SO CLEAR" TO
ANCIENT PRIESTS.

Now arrange the circled letters to form the surprise answer, as suggested by the above cartoon.

Print answer here " "

PUZZLE 47

JUMBLE®

Unscramble these four Jumbles, one letter to each square, to form four ordinary words.

SOUNDS LIKE AN APPROPRIATE PLACE FOR AN OUTDOOR POP CONCERT.

WORNC

ROGOM

NEDDAW

YELLIK

Now arrange the circled letters to form the surprise answer, as suggested by the above cartoon.

Print answer here **A**

PUZZLE 48

JUMBLE®

Unscramble these four Jumbles, one letter to each square, to form four ordinary words.

NUWDE

VORAB

PHONIS

VANDIE

WHAT THE NUDIST DEMONSTRATORS DID

Now arrange the circled letters to form the surprise answer, as suggested by the above cartoon.

Print answer here THEIR

PUZZLE 49

JUMBLE®

Unscramble these four Jumbles, one letter to each square, to form four ordinary words.

MYLIF

YOPPP

RUTUNE

DRAFIT

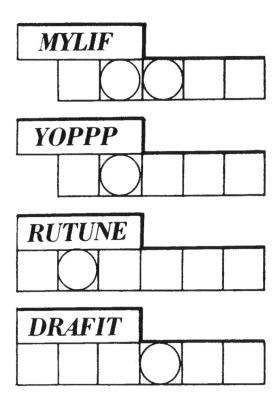

HOW TO PAINT
A SARDINE.

Now arrange the circled letters to form the surprise answer, as suggested by the above cartoon.

Print answer here

JUMBLE®

Unscramble these four Jumbles, one letter to each square, to form four ordinary words.

POCUE

KERPI

FONTIY

RELPHE

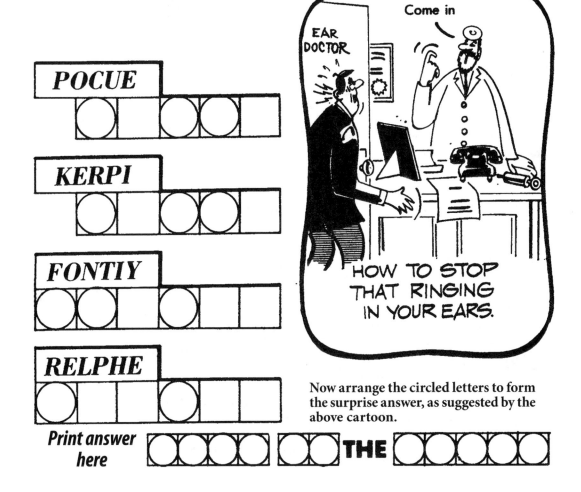

EAR DOCTOR
Come in
HOW TO STOP THAT RINGING IN YOUR EARS.

Now arrange the circled letters to form the surprise answer, as suggested by the above cartoon.

Print answer here ◯◯◯◯ ◯◯ THE ◯◯◯◯◯◯

PUZZLE 51

JUMBLE®

Unscramble these four Jumbles, one letter to each square, to form four ordinary words.

POATI

YARRA

COSHOL

THRENE

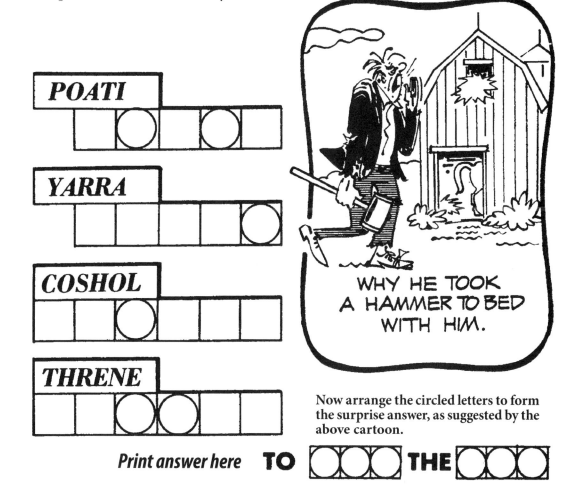

WHY HE TOOK A HAMMER TO BED WITH HIM.

Now arrange the circled letters to form the surprise answer, as suggested by the above cartoon.

Print answer here **TO** ◯◯◯ **THE** ◯◯◯

JUMBLE®

Unscramble these four Jumbles, one letter to each square, to form four ordinary words.

DIFOR

GOMEN

SPENOR

INVOIL

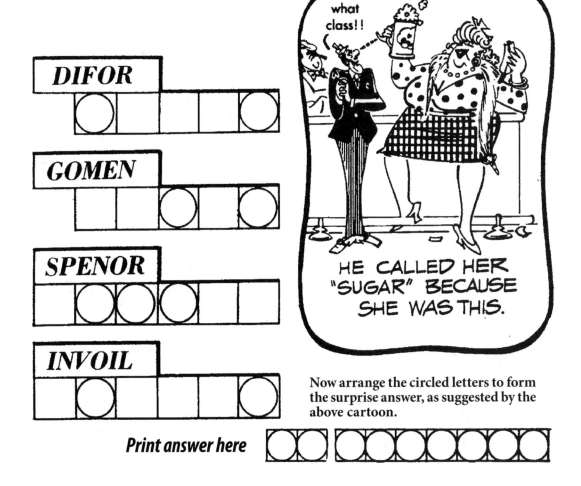

Gee—
what
class!!

HE CALLED HER "SUGAR" BECAUSE SHE WAS THIS.

Now arrange the circled letters to form the surprise answer, as suggested by the above cartoon.

Print answer here

PUZZLE 53

JUMBLE®

Unscramble these four Jumbles, one letter to each square, to form four ordinary words.

ATQUO

YITED

YALTIX

HYSERR

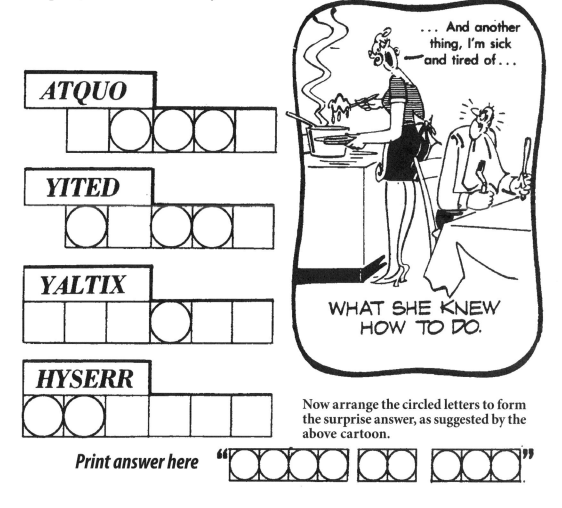

. . . And another thing, I'm sick and tired of . . .
WHAT SHE KNEW HOW TO DO.

Now arrange the circled letters to form the surprise answer, as suggested by the above cartoon.

Print answer here " "

PUZZLE 54

JUMBLE®

Unscramble these four Jumbles, one letter to each square, to form four ordinary words.

KYDUS

ADURF

TIPEOA

HAPUNC

You can't talk about the boss that way!

WHAT THE BILLPOSTER DID FOR HIS EMPLOYER.

Now arrange the circled letters to form the surprise answer, as suggested by the above cartoon.

Print answer here ⃝⃝⃝⃝⃝ ⃝⃝ ⃝⃝⃝ **HIM**

PUZZLE 55

JUMBLE®

Unscramble these four Jumbles, one letter to each square, to form four ordinary words.

DRAIP

GUNDE

ATVARC

DAYMAL

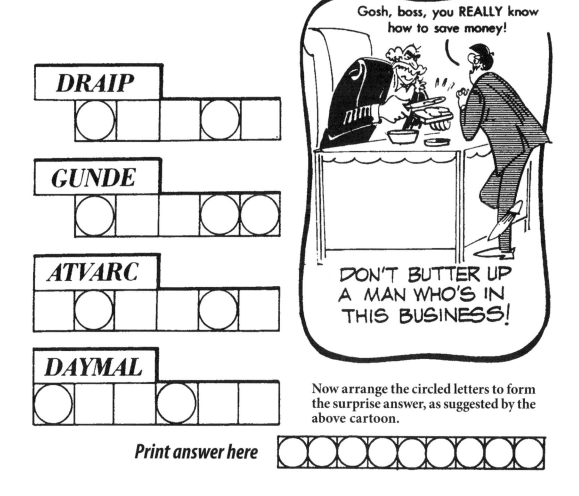

Gosh, boss, you REALLY know how to save money!
DON'T BUTTER UP A MAN WHO'S IN THIS BUSINESS!

Now arrange the circled letters to form the surprise answer, as suggested by the above cartoon.

Print answer here

PUZZLE 56

JUMBLE®

Unscramble these four Jumbles, one letter to each square, to form four ordinary words.

JYTET

GATEA

HELSIR

NAPOWE

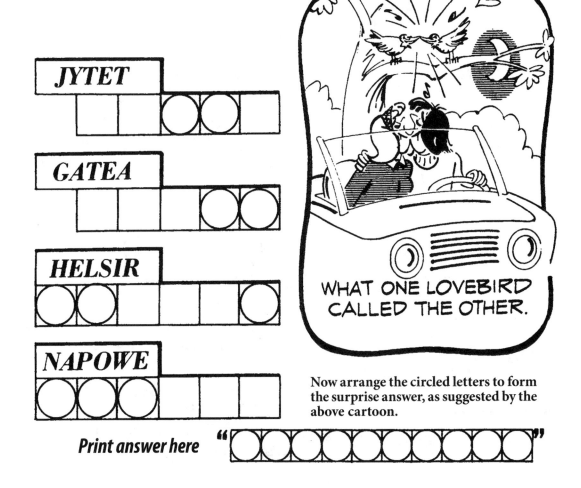

WHAT ONE LOVEBIRD CALLED THE OTHER.

Now arrange the circled letters to form the surprise answer, as suggested by the above cartoon.

Print answer here " "

PUZZLE 57

JUMBLE®

Unscramble these four Jumbles, one letter to each square, to form four ordinary words.

TILMI

USCOT

DEKBEC

EDGERD

'Hmph! My son, the mower!
WHY YOU SHOULD NEVER LET GRASS GROW UNDER YOUR FEET.

Now arrange the circled letters to form the surprise answer, as suggested by the above cartoon.

Print answer here **IT**

PUZZLE 58

JUMBLE®

Unscramble these four Jumbles, one letter to each square, to form four ordinary words.

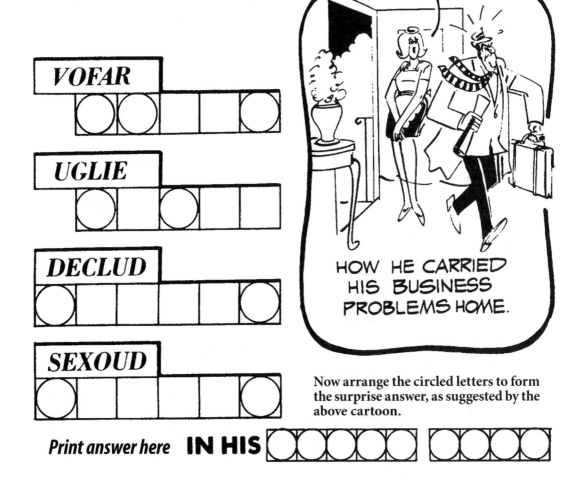

Have a nice day, dear?
HOW HE CARRIED HIS BUSINESS PROBLEMS HOME.

VOFAR

UGLIE

DECLUD

SEXOUD

Now arrange the circled letters to form the surprise answer, as suggested by the above cartoon.

Print answer here **IN HIS**

PUZZLE 59

JUMBLE®

Unscramble these four Jumbles, one letter to each square, to form four ordinary words.

NAMEG

◻ ◯ ◯ ◻ ◻

DIPAL

◻ ◯ ◻ ◯ ◻

PREEMA

◻ ◻ ◯ ◻ ◻ ◯

CAJALK

◻ ◻ ◯ ◻ ◻ ◻

SLAP!
WHERE THE USHER PUT AN OVERATTENTIVE THEATERGOER.

Now arrange the circled letters to form the surprise answer, as suggested by the above cartoon.

Print answer here ◯◯ **HIS** ◯◯◯◯◯◯

PUZZLE 60

JUMBLE®

Unscramble these four Jumbles, one letter to each square, to form four ordinary words.

OUSIP

○ ○ □ □ □

GOMAD

○ ○ □ □ □

FLUTAR

○ □ □ □ □ ○

ISSUME

□ □ ○ □ ○ □

WHAT THE GARBAGEMAN SAID HE WAS, COMPLETELY!

Now arrange the circled letters to form the surprise answer, as suggested by the above cartoon.

Print answer here **AT HER** ○○○○○○○○

PUZZLE 61

JUMBLE®

Unscramble these four Jumbles, one letter to each square, to form four ordinary words.

BYRDE

HOTUM

DINDAC

SORRAY

They'll never make the big time
COACH

AFTER A DIRTY GAME, THESE BALLPLAYERS WERE ALL WASHED UP.

Now arrange the circled letters to form the surprise answer, as suggested by the above cartoon.

Print answer here **THE**

PUZZLE 62

JUMBLE®

Unscramble these four Jumbles, one letter to each square, to form four ordinary words.

NIRAY

PRIPE

VEEBAH

HOKOUN

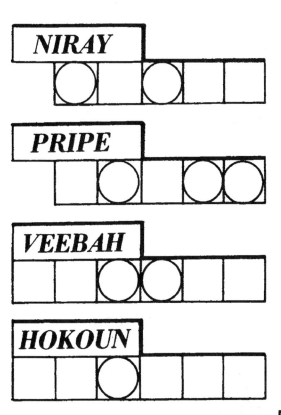

He'll be taking over

WHAT THE RICH WIGMAKER'S SON WAS.

Now arrange the circled letters to form the surprise answer, as suggested by the above cartoon.

Print answer here **THE**

JUMBLE®

Unscramble these four Jumbles, one letter to each square, to form four ordinary words.

ROATA

HUSBY

NACAMI

FERPER

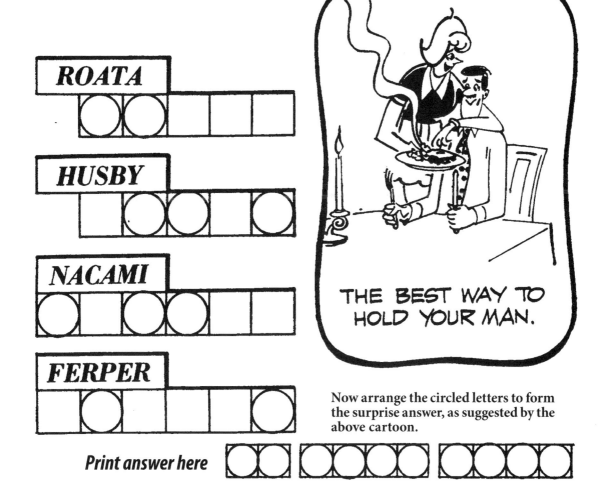

THE BEST WAY TO HOLD YOUR MAN.

Now arrange the circled letters to form the surprise answer, as suggested by the above cartoon.

Print answer here

PUZZLE 64

JUMBLE®

Unscramble these four Jumbles, one letter to each square, to form four ordinary words.

PYMUB

AFTEC

SAUNAE

CALAPA

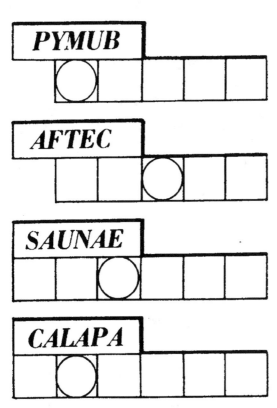

THE CAVEMAN'S FAVORITE SANDWICH.

Now arrange the circled letters to form the surprise answer, as suggested by the above cartoon.

Print answer here

PUZZLE 65

JUMBLE®

Unscramble these four Jumbles, one letter to each square, to form four ordinary words.

DABNY

KARAP

RIVLIE

HYBBUC

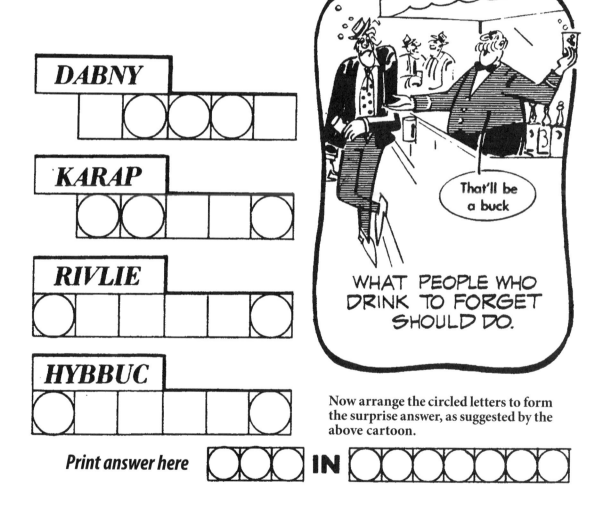

That'll be a buck
WHAT PEOPLE WHO DRINK TO FORGET SHOULD DO.

Now arrange the circled letters to form the surprise answer, as suggested by the above cartoon.

Print answer here ☐☐☐ **IN** ☐☐☐☐☐☐☐

JUMBLE®

Unscramble these four Jumbles, one letter to each square, to form four ordinary words.

BOMIL

NAVER

DORIAT

SUSTLY

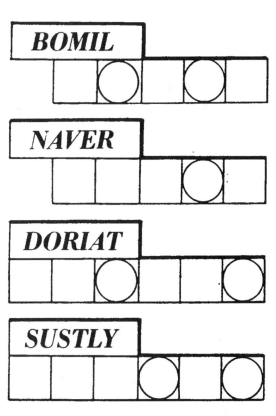

DOESN'T SHOW UP UNTIL THE WORK IS FINISHED!

Now arrange the circled letters to form the surprise answer, as suggested by the above cartoon.

Print answer here **A**

JUMBLE®

Unscramble these four Jumbles, one letter to each square, to form four ordinary words.

VOIPT

NOFET

GORFTO

TUPPIL

WHAT THE BUTTON
TYCOON WAS
ALWAYS DOING.

Now arrange the circled letters to form the surprise answer, as suggested by the above cartoon.

Print answer here

PUZZLE 68

JUMBLE®

Unscramble these four Jumbles, one letter to each square, to form four ordinary words.

FLECT

SOKYM

TOOLEC

BIRDHY

WHAT THE BALLPLAYER DID AFTER A LATE NIGHT OUT.

Now arrange the circled letters to form the surprise answer, as suggested by the above cartoon.

Print answer here " "

PUZZLE 69

JUMBLE®

Unscramble these four Jumbles, one letter to each square, to form four ordinary words.

RELIN

FLAIN

DYLOOB

STOJEL

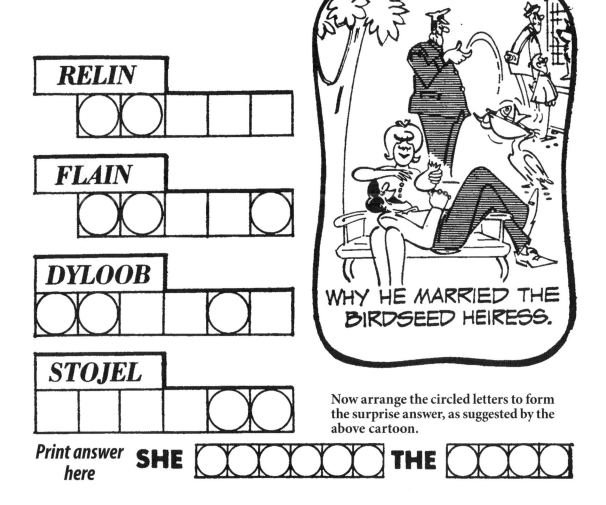

WHY HE MARRIED THE BIRDSEED HEIRESS.

Now arrange the circled letters to form the surprise answer, as suggested by the above cartoon.

Print answer here **SHE** ________ **THE** _____

PUZZLE 70

JUMBLE®

Unscramble these four Jumbles, one letter to each square, to form four ordinary words.

ZYIZD

HAABS

DEDUIG

NAANAB

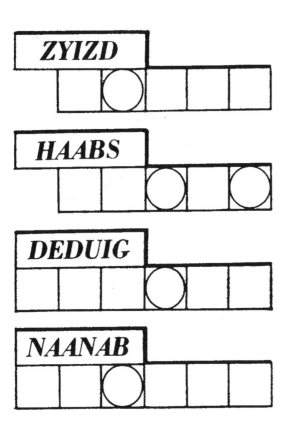

WHAT THE LUNCH WAGON OWNER NAMED HIS DAUGHTER.

Now arrange the circled letters to form the surprise answer, as suggested by the above cartoon.

Print answer here

PUZZLE 71

JUMBLE®

Unscramble these four Jumbles, one letter to each square, to form four ordinary words.

LUNCE

TYTUP

FRODIL

BEJARB

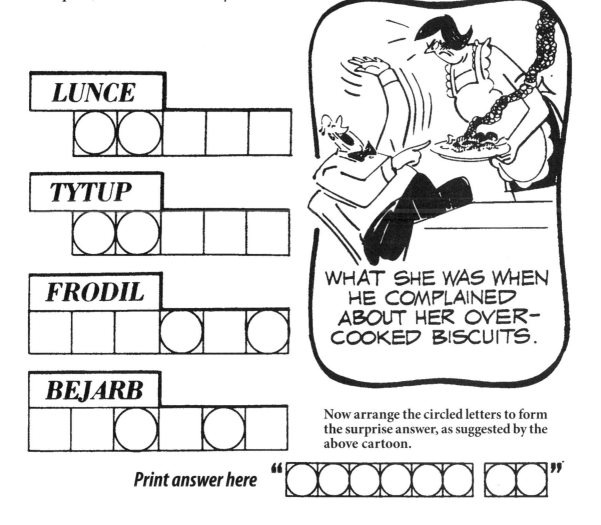

WHAT SHE WAS WHEN HE COMPLAINED ABOUT HER OVER-COOKED BISCUITS.

Now arrange the circled letters to form the surprise answer, as suggested by the above cartoon.

Print answer here “ ”

JUMBLE®

Unscramble these four Jumbles, one letter to each square, to form four ordinary words.

DOLMY

BIADE

URGETT

SVALIE

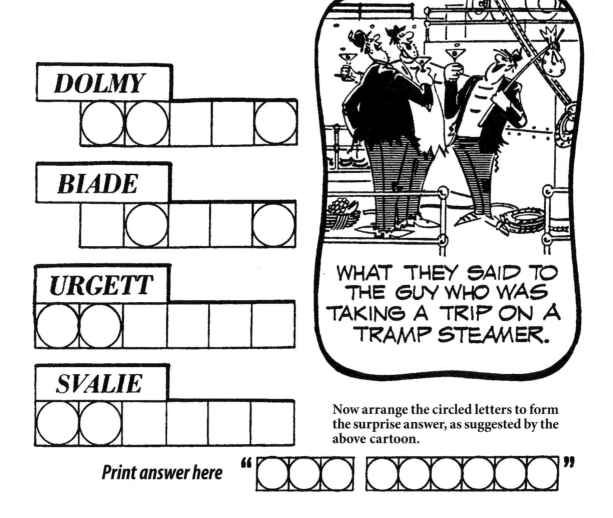

WHAT THEY SAID TO THE GUY WHO WAS TAKING A TRIP ON A TRAMP STEAMER.

Now arrange the circled letters to form the surprise answer, as suggested by the above cartoon.

Print answer here “ ”

JUMBLE®

Unscramble these four Jumbles, one letter to each square, to form four ordinary words.

PLUIP

VERAB

WORMAR

VICADE

KEEP AMERICA BEAUTIFUL
THIS MIGHT GROW IN A JUNKYARD.

Now arrange the circled letters to form the surprise answer, as suggested by the above cartoon.

Print answer here **A**

PUZZLE 74

JUMBLE®

Unscramble these four Jumbles, one letter to each square, to form four ordinary words.

YINSH

KAWTE

DIRAUM

RUPPEA

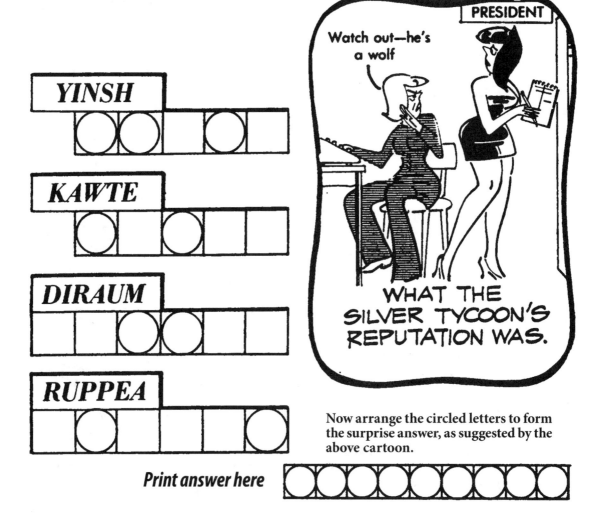

PRESIDENT
Watch out—he's a wolf

WHAT THE SILVER TYCOON'S REPUTATION WAS.

Now arrange the circled letters to form the surprise answer, as suggested by the above cartoon.

Print answer here

PUZZLE 75

JUMBLE®

Unscramble these four Jumbles, one letter to each square, to form four ordinary words.

PUTER

KIMPS

RUVESS

EIVIDD

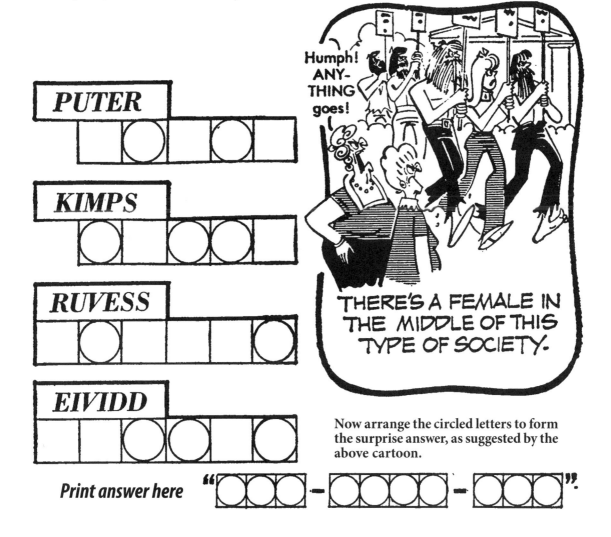

Humph! ANY- THING goes!
THERE'S A FEMALE IN THE MIDDLE OF THIS TYPE OF SOCIETY.

Now arrange the circled letters to form the surprise answer, as suggested by the above cartoon.

Print answer here "___-____-___"

JUMBLE®

Unscramble these four Jumbles, one letter to each square, to form four ordinary words.

AZIME

NOSOW

TOLBET

PERRAY

WHAT THEY MIGHT HAVE AT AN ITALIAN PICNIC.

Now arrange the circled letters to form the surprise answer, as suggested by the above cartoon.

Print answer here “○○○○-○○○○”

JUMBLE®

Unscramble these four Jumbles, one letter to each square, to form four ordinary words.

REVUC

LEVAT

TINIVE

LEWFOL

Wonderful country
FRENCH TOAST.

Now arrange the circled letters to form the surprise answer, as suggested by the above cartoon.

Print answer here ☐☐☐☐ **LA** ☐☐☐☐☐☐

JUMBLE®

Unscramble these four Jumbles, one letter to each square, to form four ordinary words.

REDEL

YELCC

NURTHE

TESSMY

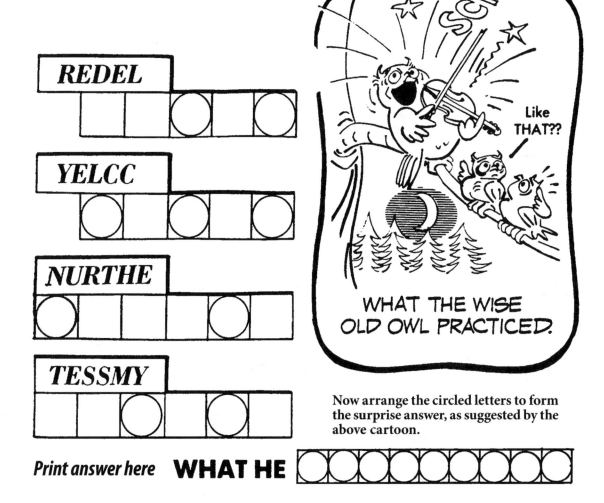

WHAT THE WISE OLD OWL PRACTICED.

Now arrange the circled letters to form the surprise answer, as suggested by the above cartoon.

Print answer here **WHAT HE**

PUZZLE 79

JUMBLE®

Unscramble these four Jumbles, one letter to each square, to form four ordinary words.

NISEG

DAUGY

SHRUPE

YAUBET

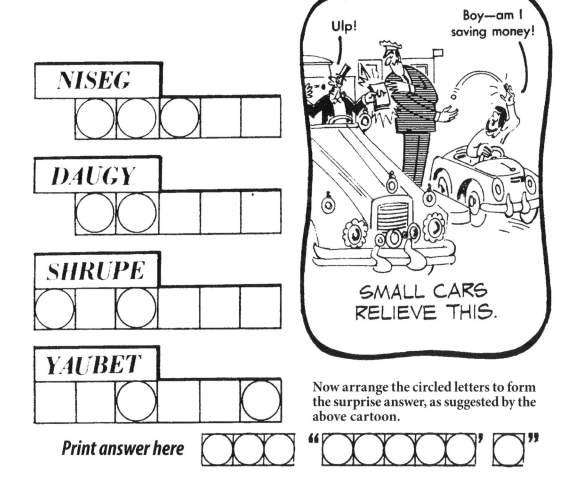

Ulp!
Boy—am I saving money!

SMALL CARS RELIEVE THIS.

Now arrange the circled letters to form the surprise answer, as suggested by the above cartoon.

Print answer here “ ’ ”

PUZZLE 80

JUMBLE®

Unscramble these four Jumbles, one letter to each square, to form four ordinary words.

TOIDI

VALAN

DRYWAT

YONNAC

Chop! Chop!
WHAT A THIRSTY MAN MIGHT DO IN FORMOSA.

Now arrange the circled letters to form the surprise answer, as suggested by the above cartoon.

Print answer here " "

JUMBLE®

Unscramble these four Jumbles, one letter to each square, to form four ordinary words.

There was this traveling salesman, see . . .
THE WOOL SALESMAN'S STOCK-IN-TRADE.

REDOO

RALNS

PUMACS

FOYFAP

Now arrange the circled letters to form the surprise answer, as suggested by the above cartoon.

Print answer here

PUZZLE 82

JUMBLE®

Unscramble these four Jumbles, one letter to each square, to form four ordinary words.

NAIGG

NAHCT

STEWEN

ZACMEE

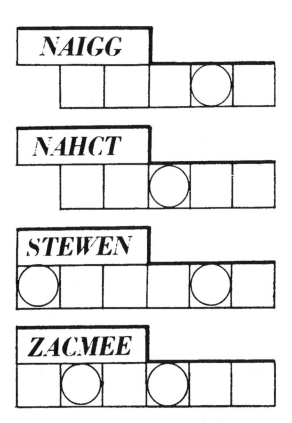

This is the place
WHERE YOU MIGHT FIND GOOD FRENCH SOUP.

Now arrange the circled letters to form the surprise answer, as suggested by the above cartoon.

Print answer here **IN** "◯◯◯◯◯◯"

PUZZLE 83

JUMBLE®

Unscramble these four Jumbles, one letter to each square, to form four ordinary words.

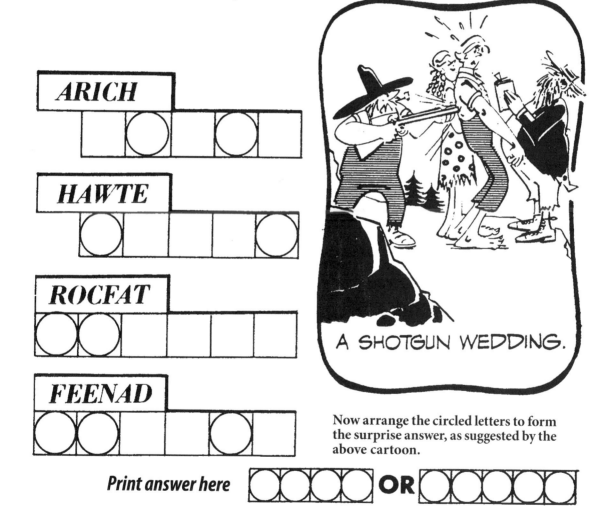

A SHOTGUN WEDDING.

ARICH

HAWTE

ROCFAT

FEENAD

Now arrange the circled letters to form the surprise answer, as suggested by the above cartoon.

Print answer here OR

JUMBLE®

Unscramble these four Jumbles, one letter to each square, to form four ordinary words.

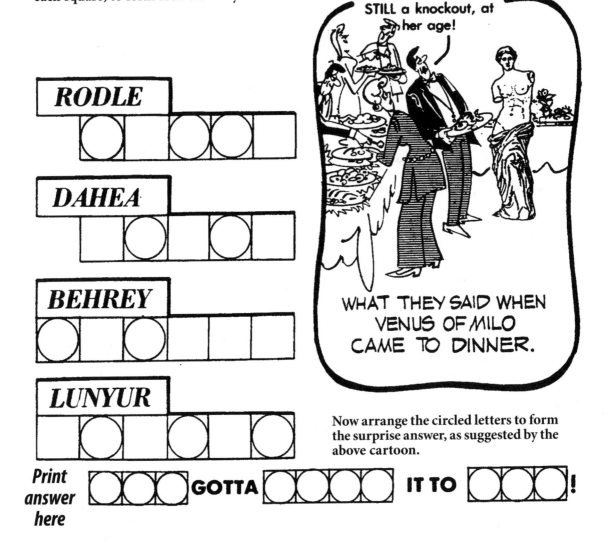

STILL a knockout, at her age!
WHAT THEY SAID WHEN VENUS OF MILO CAME TO DINNER.

RODLE

DAHEA

BEHREY

LUNYUR

Now arrange the circled letters to form the surprise answer, as suggested by the above cartoon.

Print answer here ◯◯◯ GOTTA ◯◯◯◯ IT TO ◯◯◯!

JUMBLE®

Unscramble these four Jumbles, one letter to each square, to form four ordinary words.

HAARJ

DEESU

JASTUD

YAFULT

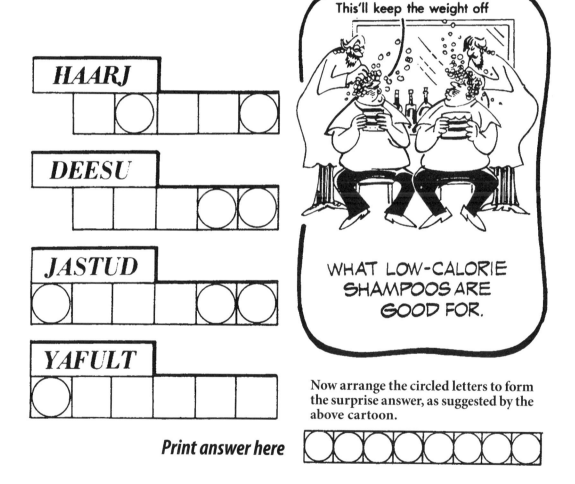

This'll keep the weight off

WHAT LOW-CALORIE SHAMPOOS ARE GOOD FOR.

Now arrange the circled letters to form the surprise answer, as suggested by the above cartoon.

Print answer here

PUZZLE 86

JUMBLE®

Unscramble these four Jumbles, one letter to each square, to form four ordinary words.

NIYKK

PRYAT

SIMPOE

CENTED

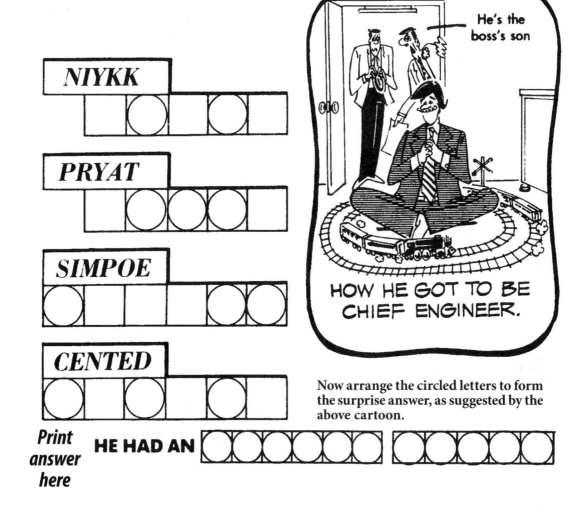

He's the boss's son
HOW HE GOT TO BE CHIEF ENGINEER.

Now arrange the circled letters to form the surprise answer, as suggested by the above cartoon.

Print answer here **HE HAD AN**

PUZZLE 87

JUMBLE®

Unscramble these four Jumbles, one letter to each square, to form four ordinary words.

YADIL

ENVOM

SHUCOR

PICTES

WHAT THEY SAID THE LADY CATTLE RANCHER HAD

Now arrange the circled letters to form the surprise answer, as suggested by the above cartoon.

Print answer here

JUMBLE®

Unscramble these four Jumbles, one letter to each square, to form four ordinary words.

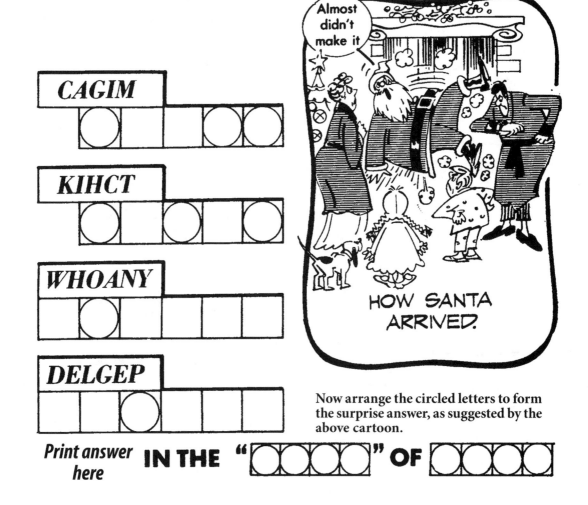

Almost didn't make it
HOW SANTA ARRIVED.

CAGIM

◯ ☐ ☐ ◯ ◯

KIHCT

◯ ☐ ◯ ☐ ◯

WHOANY

☐ ◯ ☐ ☐ ☐ ☐

DELGEP

☐ ☐ ◯ ☐ ☐ ☐

Now arrange the circled letters to form the surprise answer, as suggested by the above cartoon.

Print answer here **IN THE "◯◯◯◯◯" OF ◯◯◯◯◯**

PUZZLE 89

JUMBLE®

Unscramble these four Jumbles, one letter to each square, to form four ordinary words.

HACTY

SYNIO

RUGEDD

FLUBEM

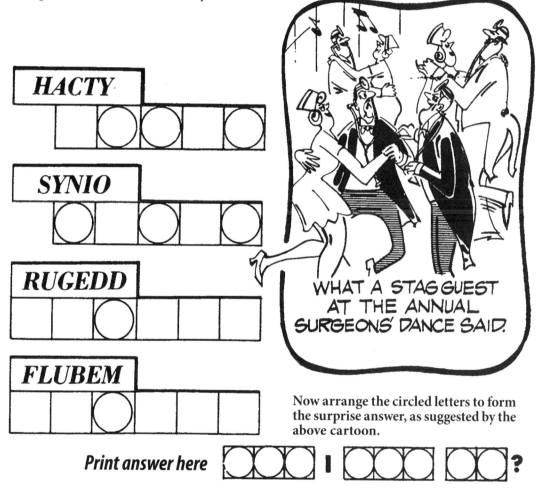

WHAT A STAG GUEST AT THE ANNUAL SURGEONS' DANCE SAID.

Now arrange the circled letters to form the surprise answer, as suggested by the above cartoon.

Print answer here ___ ! ___ ___?

PUZZLE 90

JUMBLE®

Unscramble these four Jumbles, one letter to each square, to form four ordinary words.

GLOIN

MARDA

YARDOP

LAWASY

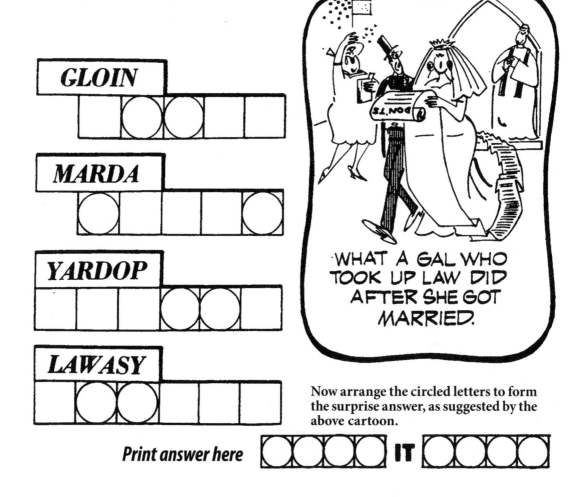

WHAT A GAL WHO TOOK UP LAW DID AFTER SHE GOT MARRIED.

Now arrange the circled letters to form the surprise answer, as suggested by the above cartoon.

Print answer here ◯◯◯◯ **IT** ◯◯◯◯◯

PUZZLE 91

JUMBLE®

Unscramble these four Jumbles, one letter to each square, to form four ordinary words.

CUNOE

HOOPT

LEGGIG

HELBED

WHAT YOU GET WHEN YOU CROSS A DOG WITH A HEN.

Now arrange the circled letters to form the surprise answer, as suggested by the above cartoon.

Print answer here **A** ______ ____

PUZZLE 92

JUMBLE®

Unscramble these four Jumbles, one letter to each square, to form four ordinary words.

CELEX

ULARR

PUDETY

DEYMEL

No water here?

WHERE THEY MIGHT PUT A MAN WHO'S BEEN CONVICTED OF ASSAULT...AND BATTERY.

Now arrange the circled letters to form the surprise answer, as suggested by the above cartoon.

Print answer here **IN A**

PUZZLE 93

JUMBLE®

Unscramble these four Jumbles, one letter to each square, to form four ordinary words.

BARRO

VENET

REBLUT

KEDONY

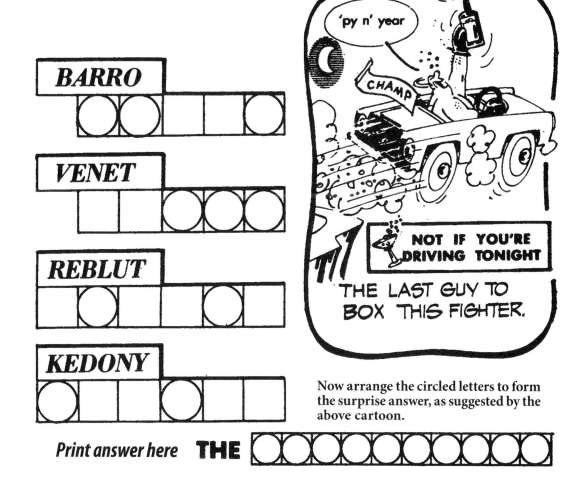

'py n' year
CHAMP
NOT IF YOU'RE DRIVING TONIGHT

THE LAST GUY TO BOX THIS FIGHTER.

Now arrange the circled letters to form the surprise answer, as suggested by the above cartoon.

Print answer here THE

PUZZLE 94

JUMBLE®

Unscramble these four Jumbles, one letter to each square, to form four ordinary words.

MULPE

USSEO

DARFIA

FLIEBE

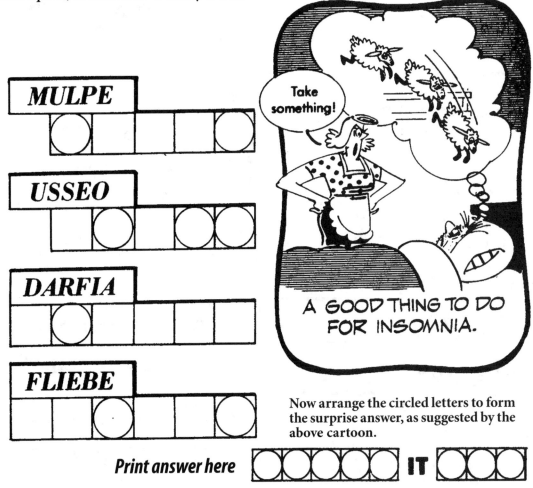

Take something!
A GOOD THING TO DO FOR INSOMNIA.

Now arrange the circled letters to form the surprise answer, as suggested by the above cartoon.

Print answer here ○○○○○ IT ○○○

PUZZLE 95

JUMBLE®

Unscramble these four Jumbles, one letter to each square, to form four ordinary words.

GOGSY

RODOB

NOOMIK

HIGLES

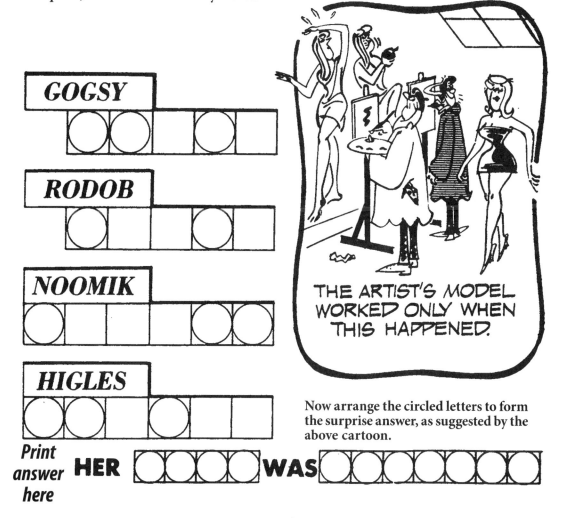

THE ARTIST'S MODEL WORKED ONLY WHEN THIS HAPPENED.

Now arrange the circled letters to form the surprise answer, as suggested by the above cartoon.

Print answer here **HER** ◯◯◯◯ **WAS** ◯◯◯◯◯◯◯

PUZZLE 96

JUMBLE®

Unscramble these four Jumbles, one letter to each square, to form four ordinary words.

OEGOS

PYNOH

TRYSOF

YANBOT

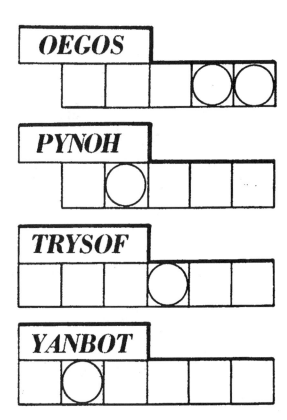

ODD IF THEY'RE BOTH RIGHT!

Now arrange the circled letters to form the surprise answer, as suggested by the above cartoon.

Print answer here

JUMBLE®

Unscramble these four Jumbles, one letter to each square, to form four ordinary words.

OPTIV

MOURF

TANDLE

AMIDDY

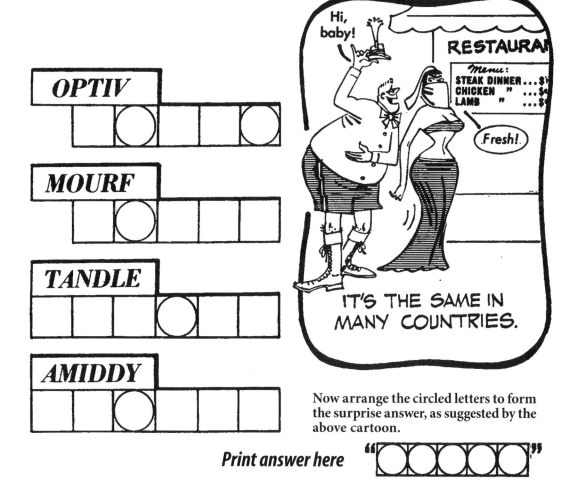

Hi, baby!
RESTAURA
Menu:
STEAK DINNER...
CHICKEN " ...
LAMB " ...
Fresh!
IT'S THE SAME IN MANY COUNTRIES.

Now arrange the circled letters to form the surprise answer, as suggested by the above cartoon.

Print answer here " "

JUMBLE®

Unscramble these four Jumbles, one letter to each square, to form four ordinary words.

DOORE

NOAPI

SCIBEP

ENMIRE

Wish I'd made this [redacted]! Then we could have retired in style
kind of money when I was young
TV REPAIR
GETS PAID AFTER HIS WORK IS FINISHED.

Now arrange the circled letters to form the surprise answer, as suggested by the above cartoon.

Print answer here **A**

PUZZLE 99

JUMBLE®

Unscramble these four Jumbles, one letter to each square, to form four ordinary words.

DONUP

POURC

LAUMSY

SHOPIN

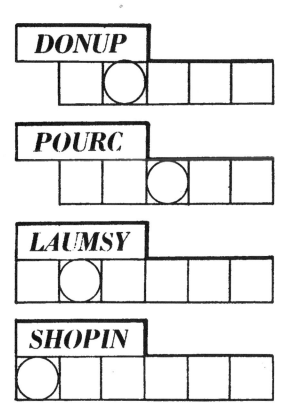

Second helping, anyone?
THIS IS NEITHER VERY GOOD NOR VERY BAD— SO, REPEAT IT!

Now arrange the circled letters to form the surprise answer, as suggested by the above cartoon.

Print answer here ☐☐-☐☐

PUZZLE 100

JUMBLE®

Unscramble these four Jumbles, one letter to each square, to form four ordinary words.

Bang!
WHY THE GUNMAN AND HIS GUN WERE DANGEROUS.

TOOPH

LIDAY

BELTOT

DRIFOL

Now arrange the circled letters to form the surprise answer, as suggested by the above cartoon.

Print answer here ◯◯◯◯ **WERE** ◯◯◯◯◯◯

PUZZLE 101

JUMBLE®

Unscramble these four Jumbles, one letter to each square, to form four ordinary words.

DEPIT

HAFFC

VAHBEE

TEGOTH

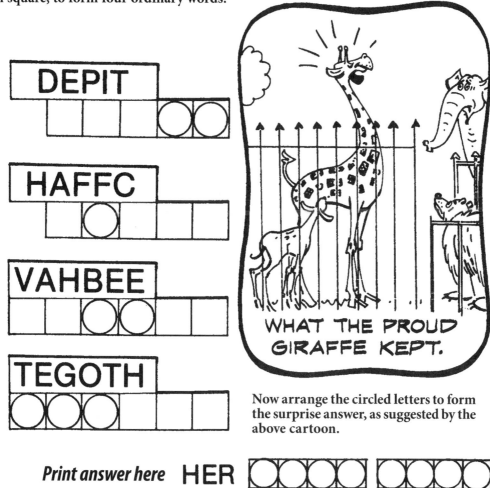

WHAT THE PROUD GIRAFFE KEPT.

Now arrange the circled letters to form the surprise answer, as suggested by the above cartoon.

Print answer here HER

JUMBLE®

Unscramble these four Jumbles, one letter to each square, to form four ordinary words.

CURUC

OEPLE

TELKIN

STEFFO

WHAT HE SAID HE WOULD DO WHEN HIS WORKERS DEMANDED A RAISE.

Now arrange the circled letters to form the surprise answer, as suggested by the above cartoon.

Print answer here ___ ___ IT

PUZZLE 103

JUMBLE®

Unscramble these four Jumbles, one letter to each square, to form four ordinary words.

YANER

◻ ◻ ◯ ◻ ◻

BICCU

◯ ◻ ◻ ◻ ◯

GROUTH

◻ ◻ ◻ ◻ ◻ ◯

TURUNE

◻ ◻ ◯ ◻ ◻ ◻

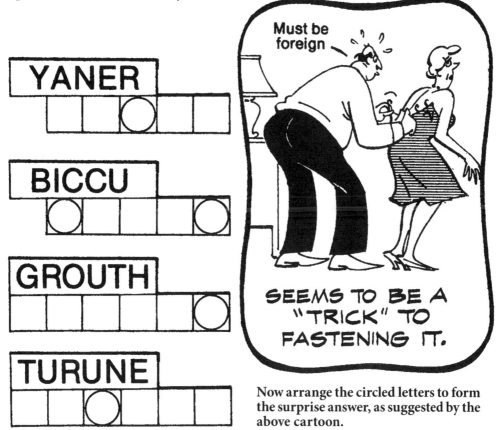

Must be foreign

SEEMS TO BE A "TRICK" TO FASTENING IT.

Now arrange the circled letters to form the surprise answer, as suggested by the above cartoon.

Print answer here A "◯◯◯◯◯"

PUZZLE 104

JUMBLE®

Unscramble these four Jumbles, one letter to each square, to form four ordinary words.

LOHLE

KERCE

NERUNG

RUSSED

POURED ON THE POLITICIAN.

Now arrange the circled letters to form the surprise answer, as suggested by the above cartoon.

Print answer here

JUMBLE®

Unscramble these four Jumbles, one letter to each square, to form four ordinary words.

ZIMEA

INBAR

DULSHO

PLESIV

Next!
WHAT THE PRETTY TATTOO ARTIST MADE ON HER CUSTOMERS.

Now arrange the circled letters to form the surprise answer, as suggested by the above cartoon.

Print answer here AN

JUMBLE®

Unscramble these four Jumbles, one letter to each square, to form four ordinary words.

ROBAR

ANUFA

YUGLIT

BACHEL

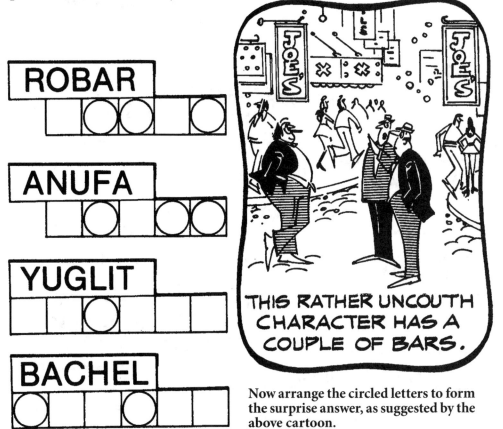

THIS RATHER UNCOUTH CHARACTER HAS A COUPLE OF BARS.

Now arrange the circled letters to form the surprise answer, as suggested by the above cartoon.

Print answer here A“ ___-___-___ ”

PUZZLE 107

JUMBLE®

Unscramble these four Jumbles, one letter to each square, to form four ordinary words.

GERME

KICCH

NEPTLY

CEERUD

WHAT YOU MIGHT LIKE THE BUTCHER TO SLICE.

Now arrange the circled letters to form the surprise answer, as suggested by the above cartoon.

Print answer here

JUMBLE®

Unscramble these four Jumbles, one letter to each square, to form four ordinary words.

KILSY

LANVA

ENMOAB

MINTIG

AM I ABLE? COULD
BE FRIENDLY!

Now arrange the circled letters to form the surprise answer, as suggested by the above cartoon.

Print answer here " "

PUZZLE 109

JUMBLE®

Unscramble these four Jumbles, one letter to each square, to form four ordinary words.

BROEP

TABEA

PHANEP

SINIST

COULD BE THE REASON—FOR HAVING MARRIED IN SPAIN.

Now arrange the circled letters to form the surprise answer, as suggested by the above cartoon.

Print answer here “ ”

PUZZLE 110

JUMBLE®

Unscramble these four Jumbles, one letter to each square, to form four ordinary words.

CHALT

YIXTS

PASHIM

BLIGET

Look! He can hardly walk!

HOW THE COPS SPOTTED THE FENCE.

Now arrange the circled letters to form the surprise answer, as suggested by the above cartoon.

Print answer here ◯◯ ◯◯◯ "◯◯◯◯◯"

JUMBLE®

Unscramble these four Jumbles, one letter to each square, to form four ordinary words.

WONGI

YERME

ZOAMAN

DROBIF

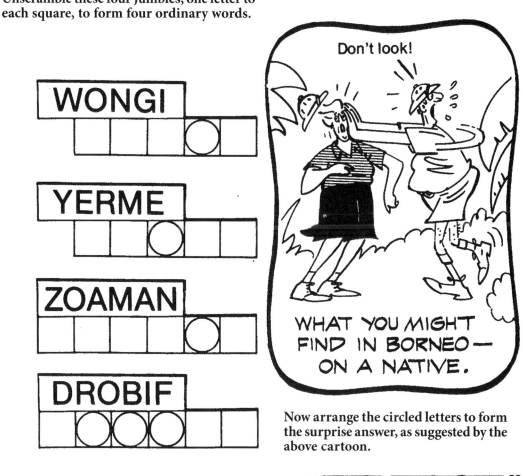

Don't look!
WHAT YOU MIGHT FIND IN BORNEO — ON A NATIVE.

Now arrange the circled letters to form the surprise answer, as suggested by the above cartoon.

Print answer here “ ”

PUZZLE 112

JUMBLE®

Unscramble these four Jumbles, one letter to each square, to form four ordinary words.

KWONN

SELLI

ODUXTE

JENTIC

WHAT HE BLAMED HIS BAD LUCK ON.

Now arrange the circled letters to form the surprise answer, as suggested by the above cartoon.

Print answer here A ____ AT THE ______

JUMBLE®

Unscramble these four Jumbles, one letter to each square, to form four ordinary words.

PINYP

DUMON

ENGALC

REEMIP

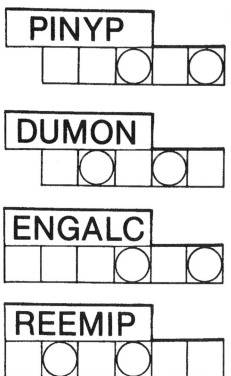

M.D.
Here, dear — you'll need a few bucks

WHAT YOU'D EXPECT TO PAY FOR AN ACUPUNCTURE TREATMENT.

Now arrange the circled letters to form the surprise answer, as suggested by the above cartoon.

Print answer here

JUMBLE®

Unscramble these four Jumbles, one letter to each square, to form four ordinary words.

CASHO

VINGE

FITHES

EXNOST

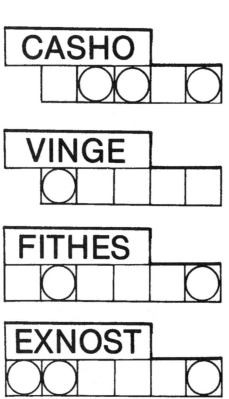

HOW AN ANGRY DENTIST GRINDS TEETH.

Now arrange the circled letters to form the surprise answer, as suggested by the above cartoon.

Print answer here

JUMBLE®

Unscramble these four Jumbles, one letter to each square, to form four ordinary words.

MIDUH

ELVOG

ICETOX

GOPINE

WHAT "TEQUILA" IS.

Now arrange the circled letters to form the surprise answer, as suggested by the above cartoon.

Print answer here THE " " OF

PUZZLE 116

JUMBLE®

Unscramble these four Jumbles, one letter to each square, to form four ordinary words.

LYMIF

OVEBA

GURTIA

KONVIE

It's all his!
WHAT HE CAME INTO WHEN HE WAS BORN.

Now arrange the circled letters to form the surprise answer, as suggested by the above cartoon.

Print answer here

PUZZLE 117

JUMBLE®

Unscramble these four Jumbles, one letter to each square, to form four ordinary words.

YASTT

TULFE

WYIHNN

GROINI

It's a flood!
THE TRAIN CARRYING THE LAUNDRYMEN TO WORK WAS DELAYED BECAUSE OF THIS.

Now arrange the circled letters to form the surprise answer, as suggested by the above cartoon.

Print answer here "☐☐☐☐☐ ☐☐☐☐" ON THE ☐☐☐☐☐

JUMBLE®

Unscramble these four Jumbles, one letter to each square, to form four ordinary words.

DAULT

ENNIL

CHOPON

FANNIT

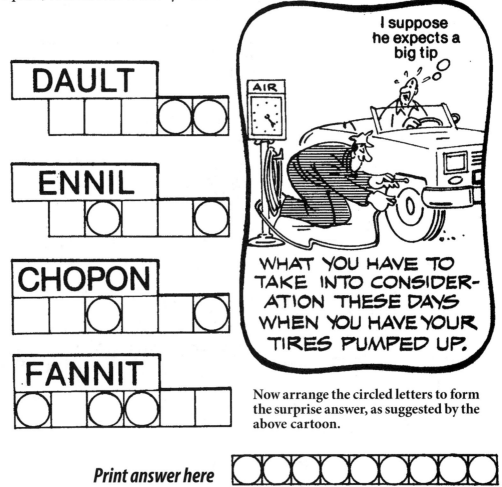

I suppose he expects a big tip
AIR
WHAT YOU HAVE TO TAKE INTO CONSIDER-ATION THESE DAYS WHEN YOU HAVE YOUR TIRES PUMPED UP.

Now arrange the circled letters to form the surprise answer, as suggested by the above cartoon.

Print answer here

JUMBLE®

Unscramble these four Jumbles, one letter to each square, to form four ordinary words.

TUBOA

SCOUF

LOOSAN

DAPRON

Now arrange the circled letters to form the surprise answer, as suggested by the above cartoon.

Print answer here " "

JUMBLE®

Unscramble these four Jumbles, one letter to each square, to form four ordinary words.

KEHRI

WHOSY

PELSOG

GOHBUT

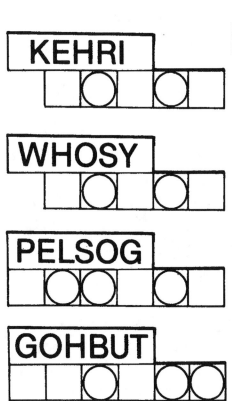

"HISTORICAL" IS THE WORD FOR THIS PRESIDENTIAL ADDRESS!

Now arrange the circled letters to form the surprise answer, as suggested by the above cartoon.

Print answer here THE

PUZZLE 121

JUMBLE®

Unscramble these four Jumbles, one letter to each square, to form four ordinary words.

SHECS

TRAFC

BROIMD

ENVARG

THREATENED TO RAIN ON THE ACTORS AT THE OUTDOOR THEATER.

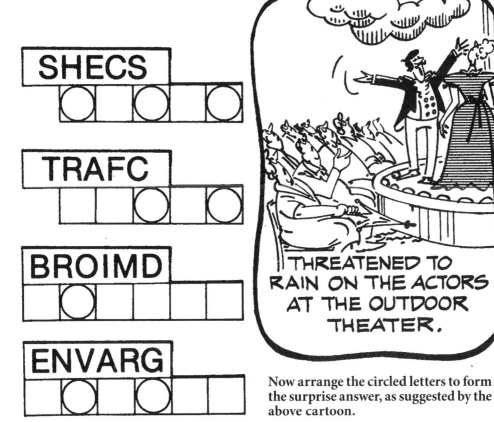

Now arrange the circled letters to form the surprise answer, as suggested by the above cartoon.

Print answer here " "

PUZZLE 122

JUMBLE®

Unscramble these four Jumbles, one letter to each square, to form four ordinary words.

WOALG

NUKKS

UPBRAL

AFDACE

Some expensive household!
BILL
ONLY ROYALTY HAVE SUCH OVERHEAD PROBLEMS.

Now arrange the circled letters to form the surprise answer, as suggested by the above cartoon.

Print answer here

PUZZLE 123

JUMBLE®

Unscramble these four Jumbles, one letter to each square, to form four ordinary words.

OPSOW

GALEL

YODMEB

BAAMEO

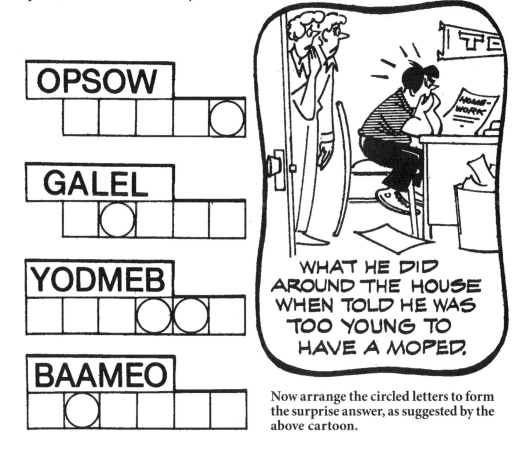

HOME-WORK
WHAT HE DID AROUND THE HOUSE WHEN TOLD HE WAS TOO YOUNG TO HAVE A MOPED.

Now arrange the circled letters to form the surprise answer, as suggested by the above cartoon.

Print answer here " "

PUZZLE 124

JUMBLE®

Unscramble these four Jumbles, one letter to each square, to form four ordinary words.

YIRDT

FETHY

JOLTES

BYRBAC

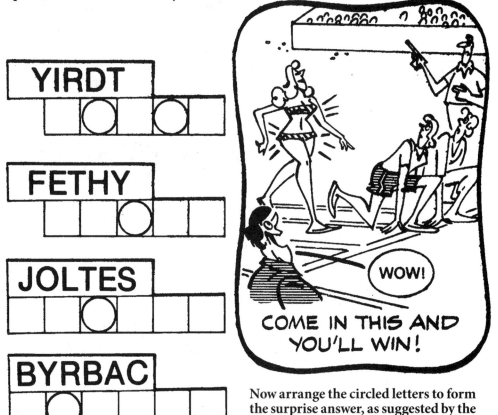

WOW!
COME IN THIS AND YOU'LL WIN!

Now arrange the circled letters to form the surprise answer, as suggested by the above cartoon.

Print answer here

JUMBLE®

Unscramble these four Jumbles, one letter to each square, to form four ordinary words.

NOAKE

SHWIK

FLUTAR

COSTAM

AGITATED WHERE COCKTAILS ARE CONCERNED.

Now arrange the circled letters to form the surprise answer, as suggested by the above cartoon.

Print answer here THE

PUZZLE 126

JUMBLE®

Unscramble these four Jumbles, one letter to each square, to form four ordinary words.

SNAIE

EWTTE

LARNAC

NAVIED

WE DEMAND OUR RIGHTS!

NOT ODD TO BE IN THE SEVENTIES!

Now arrange the circled letters to form the surprise answer, as suggested by the above cartoon.

Print answer here “ ”

PUZZLE 127

JUMBLE®

Unscramble these four Jumbles, one letter to each square, to form four ordinary words.

CUVOH

BLAWR

INREEM

ROCTAV

A BAD HABIT MIGHT GET A "GRIP" ON ONE.

Now arrange the circled letters to form the surprise answer, as suggested by the above cartoon.

Print answer here ◯ "◯◯◯◯"

PUZZLE 128

JUMBLE®

Unscramble these four Jumbles, one letter to each square, to form four ordinary words.

TURTE

DISTA

CREBIK

INTYME

HE LIKES YOU A LOT, BUT HE COULD BE MARRIED
I'll break his neck!

Now arrange the circled letters to form the surprise answer, as suggested by the above cartoon.

Print answer here " "

JUMBLE®

Unscramble these four Jumbles, one letter to each square, to form four ordinary words.

PUJEL

NADAP

HAPNOR

TIPSEC

SALE!
SALE!
WHAT BARGAIN-PRICED CAMERAS MIGHT BE.

Now arrange the circled letters to form the surprise answer, as suggested by the above cartoon.

Print answer here “ ”

JUMBLE®

Unscramble these four Jumbles, one letter to each square, to form four ordinary words.

LEWJE

DYPET

SIFOSY

BERROK

FOR THOSE WHO TRAIN BY NIGHT.

Now arrange the circled letters to form the surprise answer, as suggested by the above cartoon.

Print answer here

PUZZLE 131

JUMBLE®

Unscramble these four Jumbles, one letter to each square, to form four ordinary words.

ECHLE

DEKIN

ENCOBA

TUSALE

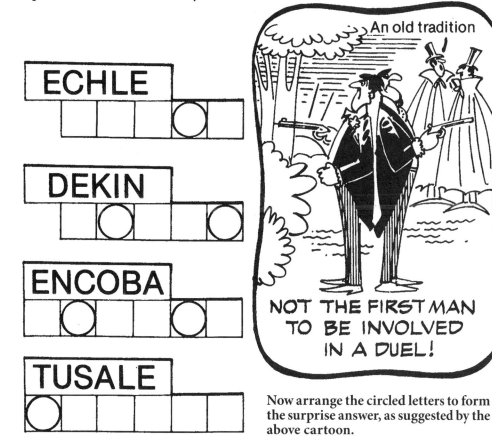

An old tradition

NOT THE FIRST MAN TO BE INVOLVED IN A DUEL!

Now arrange the circled letters to form the surprise answer, as suggested by the above cartoon.

Print answer here THE

PUZZLE 132

JUMBLE®

Unscramble these four Jumbles, one letter to each square, to form four ordinary words.

HIWSS

ENPOY

NENKLE

MODEOD

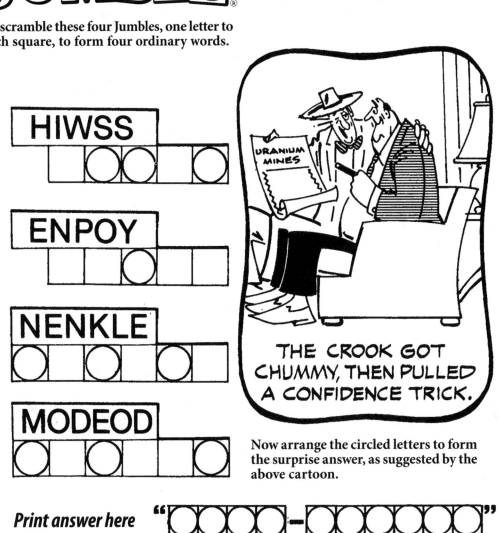

THE CROOK GOT CHUMMY, THEN PULLED A CONFIDENCE TRICK.

Now arrange the circled letters to form the surprise answer, as suggested by the above cartoon.

Print answer here "____-______"

PUZZLE 133

JUMBLE®

Unscramble these four Jumbles, one letter to each square, to form four ordinary words.

EGGAU

TAFOO

INCADD

GROOFT

RATHER OLD-FASHIONED —BUT MANAGED TO GO OUT WITH BOYS NEVERTHELESS.

Now arrange the circled letters to form the surprise answer, as suggested by the above cartoon.

Print answer here " "

PUZZLE 134

JUMBLE®

Unscramble these four Jumbles, one letter to each square, to form four ordinary words.

SPAWM

HORTT

DULANO

BELMAG

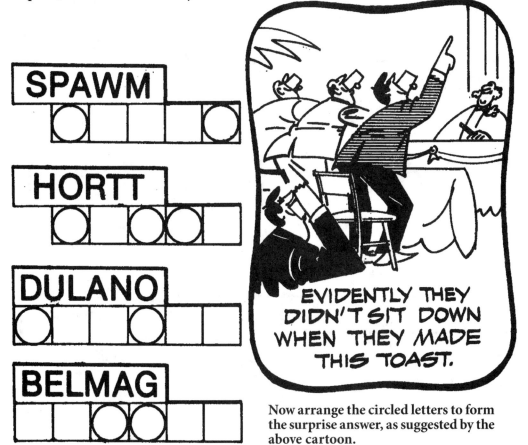

EVIDENTLY THEY DIDN'T SIT DOWN WHEN THEY MADE THIS TOAST.

Now arrange the circled letters to form the surprise answer, as suggested by the above cartoon.

Print answer here " "

JUMBLE®

Unscramble these four Jumbles, one letter to each square, to form four ordinary words.

THEFC

YALFE

CEVIED

DANNIL

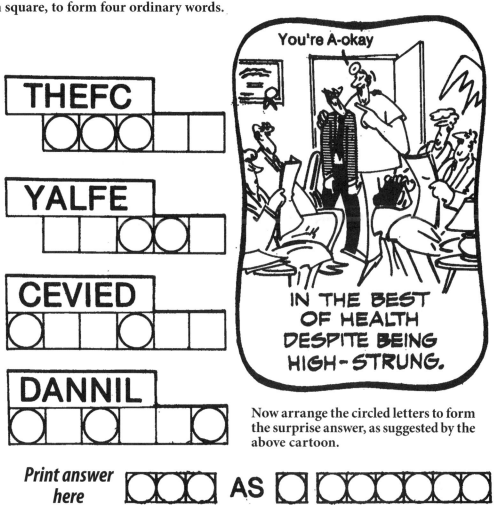

You're A-okay
IN THE BEST OF HEALTH DESPITE BEING HIGH-STRUNG.

Now arrange the circled letters to form the surprise answer, as suggested by the above cartoon.

Print answer here ☐☐☐ AS ☐ ☐☐☐☐☐☐

JUMBLE®

Unscramble these four Jumbles, one letter to each square, to form four ordinary words.

CLUNE

IXOCT

NOMCOM

TOXREV

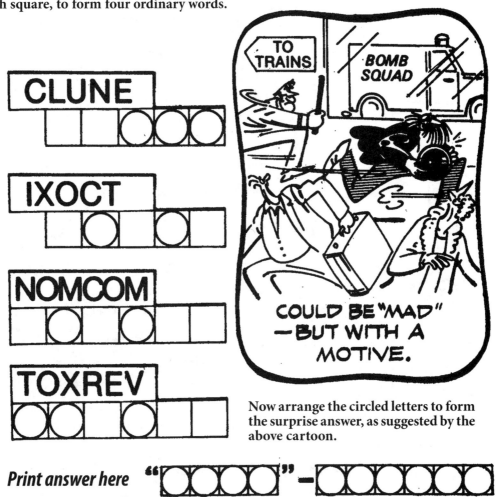

COULD BE "MAD" —BUT WITH A MOTIVE.

Now arrange the circled letters to form the surprise answer, as suggested by the above cartoon.

Print answer here " " –

PUZZLE 137

JUMBLE®

Unscramble these four Jumbles, one letter to each square, to form four ordinary words.

YOHAR

TUFOL

SHULOC

GOULEY

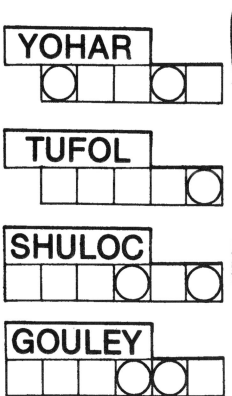

That does it!
LOVE THY NEIGHBOR
WHAT HE WAS WHEN HE WAS FINISHED WITH THE DRILLING.

Now arrange the circled letters to form the surprise answer, as suggested by the above cartoon.

Print answer here “ ”

JUMBLE®

Unscramble these four Jumbles, one letter to each square, to form four ordinary words.

KULFE

GLARN

NINTTE

BIEFLE

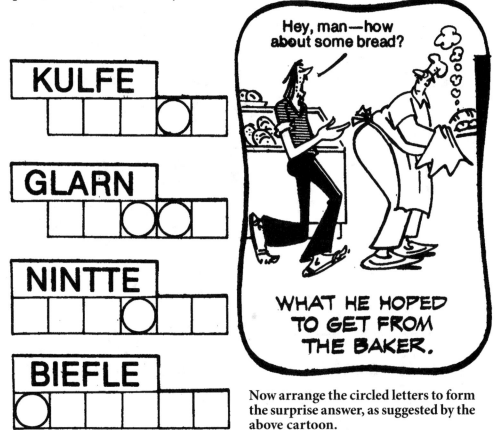

Hey, man—how about some bread?
WHAT HE HOPED TO GET FROM THE BAKER.

Now arrange the circled letters to form the surprise answer, as suggested by the above cartoon.

Print answer here **A** " "

JUMBLE®

Unscramble these four Jumbles, one letter to each square, to form four ordinary words.

TENIL

ORXYP

MEUGLE

DERAIV

AM PLEASED TO HAVE ENOUGH TO START WITH
Your appetizer, sir

Now arrange the circled letters to form the surprise answer, as suggested by the above cartoon.

Print answer here " "

JUMBLE®

Unscramble these four Jumbles, one letter to each square, to form four ordinary words.

THICY

ICCOL

YARNEL

SLIMIE

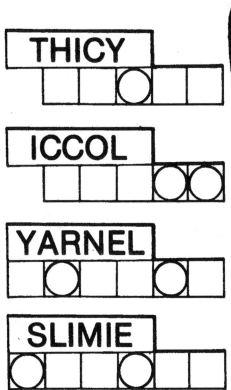

THEY OFTEN HANG ABOUT IN THE COLD.

Now arrange the circled letters to form the surprise answer, as suggested by the above cartoon.

Print answer here

PUZZLE 141

JUMBLE®

Unscramble these four Jumbles, one letter to each square, to form four ordinary words.

EUDLE

GUGOE

NEDDAW

CAGNEY

'Tis nothin'!
WHAT A HEARTY SCOTSMAN MIGHT CON-SIDER A SEVEN-DAY CASE OF THE FLU.

Now arrange the circled letters to form the surprise answer, as suggested by the above cartoon.

Print answer here JUST A

JUMBLE®

Unscramble these four Jumbles, one letter to each square, to form four ordinary words.

YORRS

BAYBE

CLYMAL

OPTATE

ACME DYNAMITE WORKS
MORE orders!
A SOUND INCREASE IN BUSINESS.

Now arrange the circled letters to form the surprise answer, as suggested by the above cartoon.

Print answer here ◯◯◯◯!

JUMBLE®

Unscramble these four Jumbles, one letter to each square, to form four ordinary words.

PLIMB

CRAID

TEMNEC

RELPHE

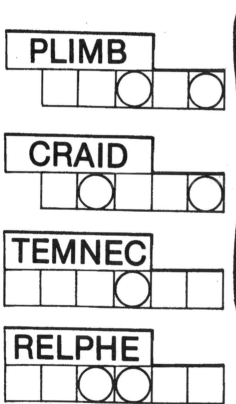

That'll be $100, sir

WHAT HE GOT WHEN HE WENT TO ONE OF THOSE "HIGH-CLASS" HAIR STYLISTS.

Now arrange the circled letters to form the surprise answer, as suggested by the above cartoon.

Print answer here " "

PUZZLE 144

JUMBLE®

Unscramble these four Jumbles, one letter to each square, to form four ordinary words.

KLEAY

☐ ☐ ◯ ☐ ☐

DAMEF

☐ ☐ ◯ ☐ ◯

CABEEM

☐ ☐ ◯ ☐ ☐ ◯

VOLJIA

☐ ☐ ☐ ◯ ☐ ◯

COULD BE CLAIMED— TO BE A MATTER FOR THE DOCTOR.

Now arrange the circled letters to form the surprise answer, as suggested by the above cartoon.

Print answer here "◯◯◯◯◯◯◯"

PUZZLE 145

JUMBLE®

Unscramble these four Jumbles, one letter to each square, to form four ordinary words.

RECEL

GOGSY

YEASUN

DUGIED

EVEN BETTER THAN
A CLOSE FRIEND.

Now arrange the circled letters to form the surprise answer, as suggested by the above cartoon.

Print answer here A ◯◯◯◯◯◯◯◯◯ ONE

JUMBLE®

Unscramble these four Jumbles, one letter to each square, to form four ordinary words.

YUINF

GEMAL

DEVAHL

CLUSIE

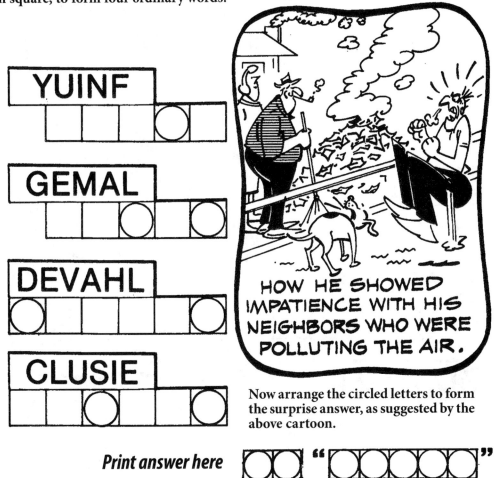

HOW HE SHOWED IMPATIENCE WITH HIS NEIGHBORS WHO WERE POLLUTING THE AIR.

Now arrange the circled letters to form the surprise answer, as suggested by the above cartoon.

Print answer here ◯◯ "◯◯◯◯◯◯"

PUZZLE 147

JUMBLE®

Unscramble these four Jumbles, one letter to each square, to form four ordinary words.

GALOT

KANCK

DIPALL

NAILET

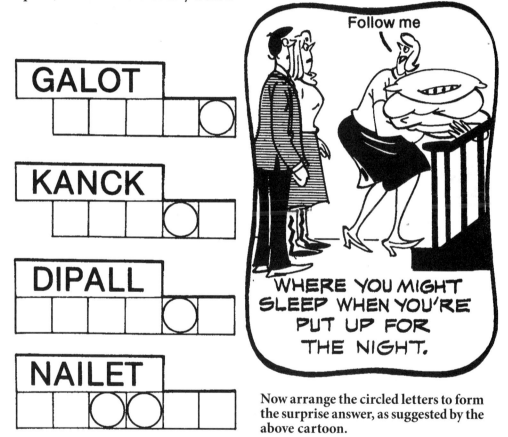

Follow me
WHERE YOU MIGHT SLEEP WHEN YOU'RE PUT UP FOR THE NIGHT.

Now arrange the circled letters to form the surprise answer, as suggested by the above cartoon.

Print answer here THE

PUZZLE **148**

JUMBLE®

Unscramble these four Jumbles, one letter to each square, to form four ordinary words.

HUBSY

DYRYL

TASHAG

BEFLAD

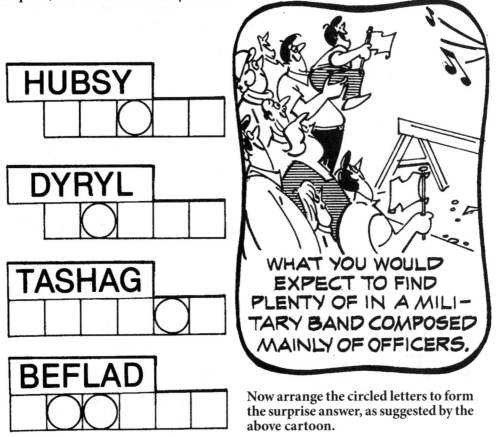

WHAT YOU WOULD EXPECT TO FIND PLENTY OF IN A MILI- TARY BAND COMPOSED MAINLY OF OFFICERS.

Now arrange the circled letters to form the surprise answer, as suggested by the above cartoon.

Print answer here “ ”

JUMBLE®

Unscramble these four Jumbles, one letter to each square, to form four ordinary words.

YIZZD

DEEXU

FIGNAC

ENBODY

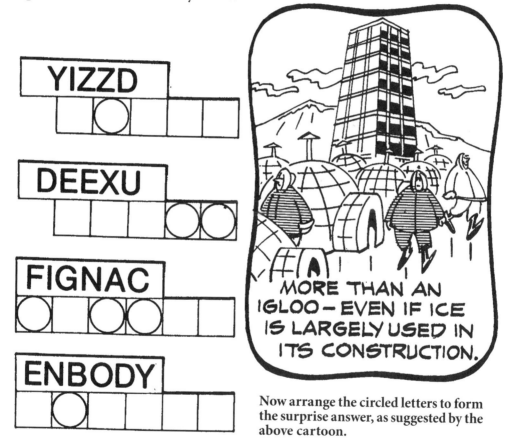

MORE THAN AN IGLOO — EVEN IF ICE IS LARGELY USED IN ITS CONSTRUCTION.

Now arrange the circled letters to form the surprise answer, as suggested by the above cartoon.

Print answer here "◯◯-◯◯-◯◯◯"

PUZZLE 150

JUMBLE®

Unscramble these four Jumbles, one letter to each square, to form four ordinary words.

SOUMY

KOBOR

TRIEHD

GALEGH

WHAT THE DERMATOLOGIST'S BEHAVIOR WAS, TO SAY THE LEAST.

Now arrange the circled letters to form the surprise answer, as suggested by the above cartoon.

Print answer here " "

JUMBLE®

Unscramble these four Jumbles, one letter to each square, to form four ordinary words.

TEGOB

KECAD

MIKOON

NAHDEL

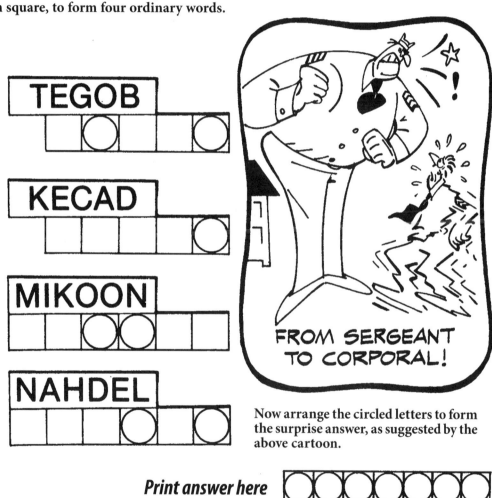

FROM SERGEANT TO CORPORAL!

Now arrange the circled letters to form the surprise answer, as suggested by the above cartoon.

Print answer here

PUZZLE 152

JUMBLE®

Unscramble these four Jumbles, one letter to each square, to form four ordinary words.

GURAU

SHLYP

KLAYEC

ZAHDAR

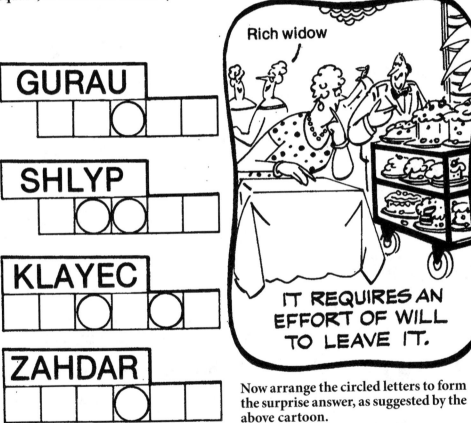

IT REQUIRES AN EFFORT OF WILL TO LEAVE IT.

Now arrange the circled letters to form the surprise answer, as suggested by the above cartoon.

Print answer here A ◯◯◯◯◯◯

PUZZLE 153

JUMBLE®

Unscramble these four Jumbles, one letter to each square, to form four ordinary words.

GEFUD

VANKE

LATHEC

FLUNGE

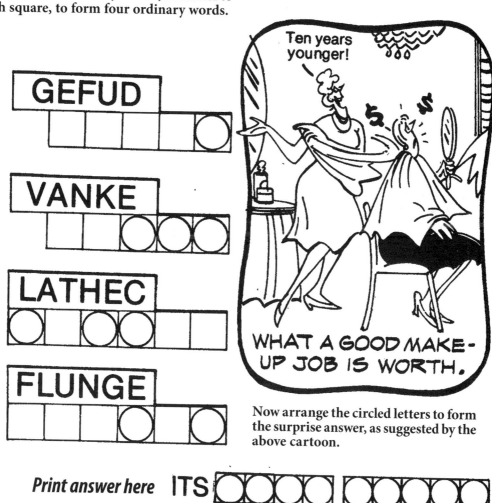

Ten years younger!
WHAT A GOOD MAKE-UP JOB IS WORTH.

Now arrange the circled letters to form the surprise answer, as suggested by the above cartoon.

Print answer here ITS

JUMBLE®

Unscramble these four Jumbles, one letter to each square, to form four ordinary words.

ORSAL

HOALT

TRIMOP

GLEENT

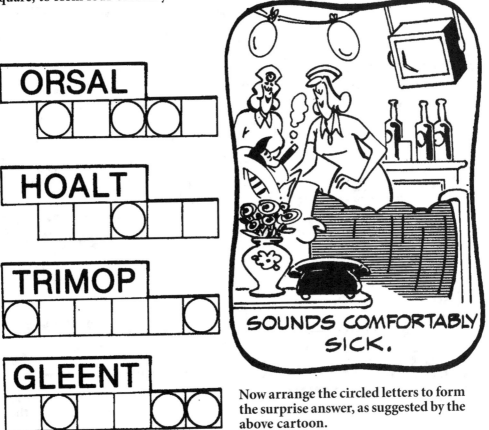

SOUNDS COMFORTABLY SICK.

Now arrange the circled letters to form the surprise answer, as suggested by the above cartoon.

Print answer here " "

JUMBLE®

Unscramble these four Jumbles, one letter to each square, to form four ordinary words.

WYSON

TELOX

CEPPIT

LAMDAY

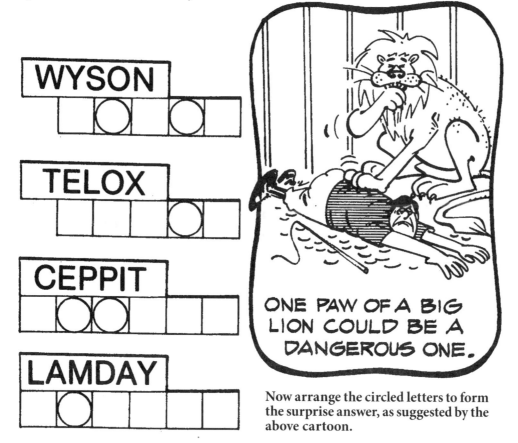

ONE PAW OF A BIG LION COULD BE A DANGEROUS ONE.

Now arrange the circled letters to form the surprise answer, as suggested by the above cartoon.

Print answer here " "

PUZZLE 156

JUMBLE®

Unscramble these four Jumbles, one letter to each square, to form four ordinary words.

REVNY

JEGUD

GUYSAR

FACSIO

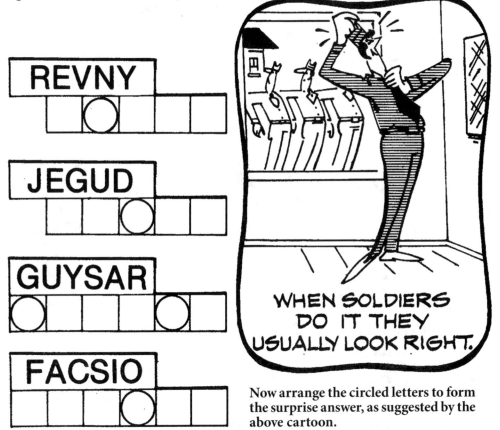

WHEN SOLDIERS DO IT THEY USUALLY LOOK RIGHT.

Now arrange the circled letters to form the surprise answer, as suggested by the above cartoon.

Print answer here “ ”

PUZZLE 157

JUMBLE®

Unscramble these four Jumbles, one letter to each square, to form four ordinary words.

LUTEX

BOVAR

DIASUN

TEESHE

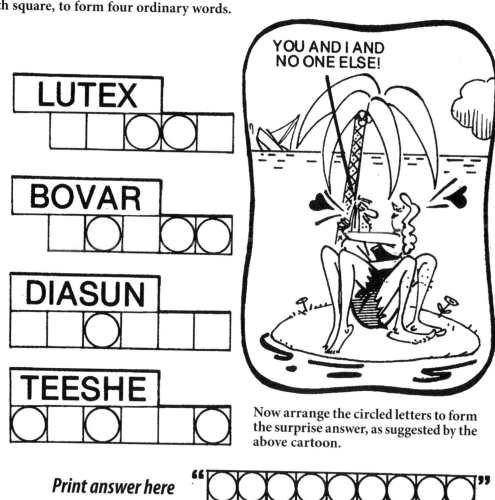

YOU AND I AND NO ONE ELSE!

Now arrange the circled letters to form the surprise answer, as suggested by the above cartoon.

Print answer here “ ”

JUMBLE®

Unscramble these four Jumbles, one letter to each square, to form four ordinary words.

ORVAS

TINGY

TOCCUL

CELFIK

Sign here!
SHRINK FROM A BUSINESS DEAL.

Now arrange the circled letters to form the surprise answer, as suggested by the above cartoon.

Print answer here " "

JUMBLE®

Unscramble these four Jumbles, one letter to each square, to form four ordinary words.

JOGIN

BLEEL

STYLUB

RAKNEC

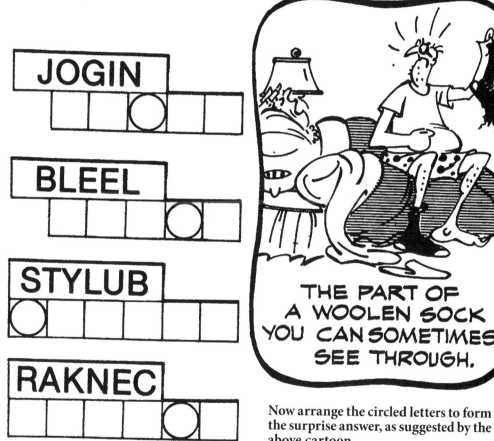

THE PART OF
A WOOLEN SOCK
YOU CAN SOMETIMES
SEE THROUGH.

Now arrange the circled letters to form the surprise answer, as suggested by the above cartoon.

Print answer here " "

PUZZLE 160

JUMBLE®

Unscramble these four Jumbles, one letter to each square, to form four ordinary words.

KIMPS

BYRIN

EXVONC

NUCHAH

Aren't you supposed to be cleaning out the garage?
POEMS
WHAT TIME AND GRIME DO.

Now arrange the circled letters to form the surprise answer, as suggested by the above cartoon.

Print answer here

JUMBLE® KNOCKOUT

Challenger Puzzles

JUMBLE®

Unscramble these six Jumbles, one letter to each square, to form six ordinary words.

INDATE

BOCIXE

GOAFER

ELBARR

CHOTLE

DELNAH

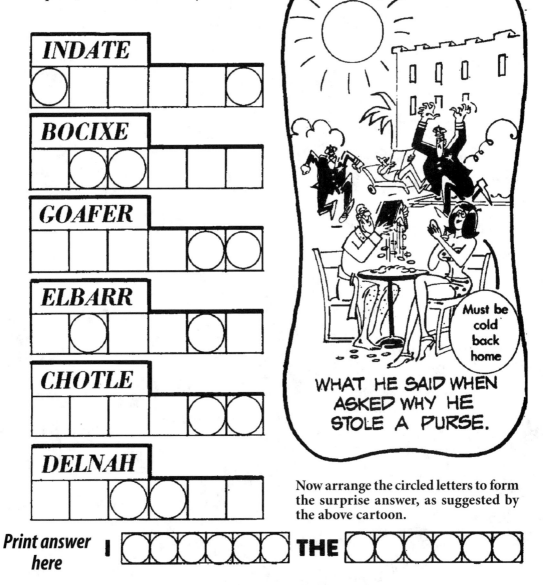

Must be cold back home

WHAT HE SAID WHEN ASKED WHY HE STOLE A PURSE.

Now arrange the circled letters to form the surprise answer, as suggested by the above cartoon.

Print answer here **I** ◯◯◯◯◯◯ **THE** ◯◯◯◯◯◯

PUZZLE 162

JUMBLE®

Unscramble these six Jumbles, one letter to each square, to form six ordinary words.

NABYRD

GAAMED

CLIPES

DULCOY

TANFIN

WEVILS

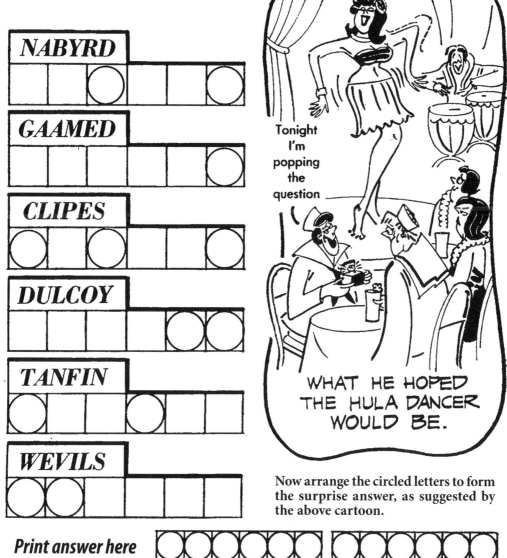

Tonight I'm popping the question
WHAT HE HOPED THE HULA DANCER WOULD BE.

Now arrange the circled letters to form the surprise answer, as suggested by the above cartoon.

Print answer here

PUZZLE 163

JUMBLE®

Unscramble these six Jumbles, one letter to each square, to form six ordinary words.

YELMPO

SAUCCU

NEDGER

TEBICS

TOCIPE

IBBART

How do you expect a guy to work when he's hungry?
WHY GOOD AUTHORS NEVER WRITE ON AN EMPTY STOMACH.

Now arrange the circled letters to form the surprise answer, as suggested by the above cartoon.

Print answer here

PUZZLE 164

JUMBLE®

Unscramble these six Jumbles, one letter to each square, to form six ordinary words.

PASTEC

THOGTE

DOWMIS

FLERBY

LONPEL

BAACAN

Darn!
WHY THE VAMPIRE AVOIDED HER.

Now arrange the circled letters to form the surprise answer, as suggested by the above cartoon.

Print answer here

PUZZLE 165

JUMBLE®

Unscramble these six Jumbles, one letter to each square, to form six ordinary words.

ROCENE

TEETIP

PHOSUT

MEEDAF

FRILPE

ABNERN

$
NO MATTER HOW EARLY THE JUDGE STARTED WORK, HE ALWAYS FOUND THIS.

Now arrange the circled letters to form the surprise answer, as suggested by the above cartoon.

Print answer here HIM.

JUMBLE®

Unscramble these six Jumbles, one letter to each square, to form six ordinary words.

GLARAN

MORRAY

BUNNIO

MYSLOB

LIFTLE

IMMORE

BEER
Where to now?
A METRONOME CAN DETERMINE THE SPEED WITH WHICH YOU GO—

Now arrange the circled letters to form the surprise answer, as suggested by the above cartoon.

Print answer here

PUZZLE 167

JUMBLE®

Unscramble these six Jumbles, one letter to each square, to form six ordinary words.

TOESGO

PLUXED

CARCIT

RAYTLE

DROINO

GLYFAD

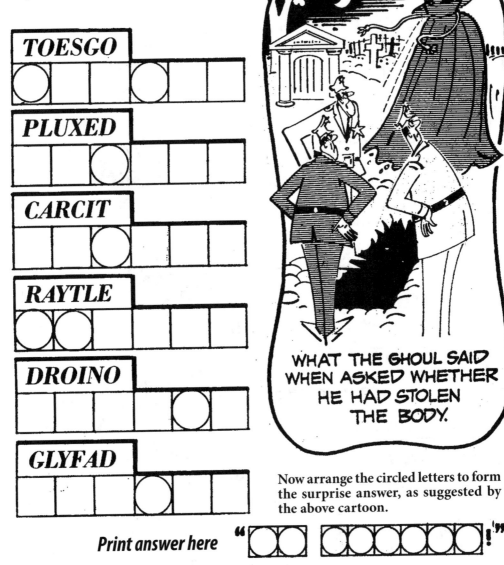

WHAT THE GHOUL SAID WHEN ASKED WHETHER HE HAD STOLEN THE BODY.

Now arrange the circled letters to form the surprise answer, as suggested by the above cartoon.

Print answer here "◯◯ ◯◯◯◯◯◯!"

JUMBLE®

Unscramble these six Jumbles, one letter to each square, to form six ordinary words.

SPOLGE

RIELOO

BOTHED

UNRATT

YIRAWA

BEEKAT

AN ALARM CLOCK CAN SCARE THIS.

Now arrange the circled letters to form the surprise answer, as suggested by the above cartoon.

Print answer here THE ○○○○○○○○ ○○○○ YOU

JUMBLE®

Unscramble these six Jumbles, one letter to each square, to form six ordinary words.

BERROK

NILJEG

DRATOW

CUDLAN

BOLIFE

PONCAY

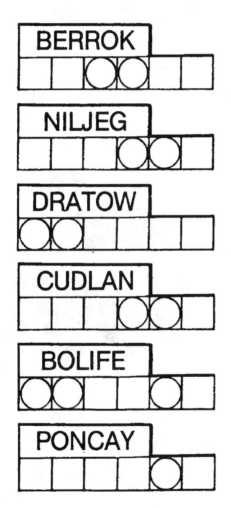

That's exactly right
Three cheers for the red, white and blue

HOW BETSY ROSS KNEW WHAT THE FOUNDING FATHERS WANTED.

Now arrange the circled letters to form the surprise answer, as suggested by the above cartoon.

Print answer here SHE ◯◯◯◯ A ◯◯◯◯ "◯◯◯◯"

PUZZLE 170

JUMBLE®

Unscramble these six Jumbles, one letter to each square, to form six ordinary words.

ACLOSE

MOUPID

HARANG

CRENOR

FILTUP

YATAPH

WHAT THEY CALLED THE GAL WHO MARRIED A LONG-HAIRED GUY IN MISSISSIPPI.

Now arrange the circled letters to form the surprise answer, as suggested by the above cartoon.

Print answer here

PUZZLE 171

JUMBLE®

Unscramble these six Jumbles, one letter to each square, to form six ordinary words.

CHUGAT

TRIMOP

ASCUBA

EMORTH

SOYSIF

TOOSHE

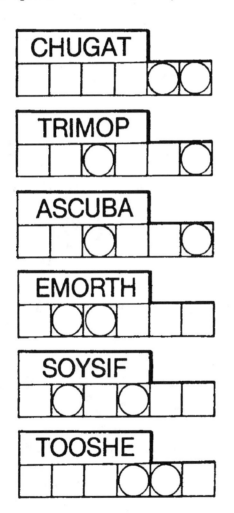

WHAT THE LEOPARD SAID WHEN HE FINISHED HIS DINNER.

Now arrange the circled letters to form the surprise answer, as suggested by the above cartoon.

Print answer here ○○○○ ○○○ THE ○○○○○

PUZZLE 172

JUMBLE®

Unscramble these six Jumbles, one letter to each square, to form six ordinary words.

ANGAME

CHELEK

BORDIF

NURULC

LAASSI

CORBON

WHAT HE GOT WHEN HE PICKED A FOUR-LEAF CLOVER GROWING IN THE MIDST OF ALL THAT POISON IVY.

Now arrange the circled letters to form the surprise answer, as suggested by the above cartoon.

Print answer here A ◯◯◯◯ OF ◯◯◯◯ ◯◯◯◯

PUZZLE 173

JUMBLE®

Unscramble these six Jumbles, one letter to each square, to form six ordinary words.

THENUR

NOGIBB

MYPLOC

TEAREA

HUDOLS

DOBCIE

You'll have to get in line
WHAT SOMEONE DID TO THE THIRSTY BOXER.

Now arrange the circled letters to form the surprise answer, as suggested by the above cartoon.

Print answer here ____ ___ TO THE “______”

JUMBLE®

Unscramble these six Jumbles, one letter to each square, to form six ordinary words.

CURPES

JEDGAG

LICTIE

ZULZEG

YUNCAL

SMOIGE

WHY SOME COUPLES GO TO "COURT."

Now arrange the circled letters to form the surprise answer, as suggested by the above cartoon.

Print answer here TO ◯◯◯◯ "◯◯◯◯◯◯◯"

PUZZLE 175

JUMBLE®

Unscramble these six Jumbles, one letter to each square, to form six ordinary words.

ENTGAM

GROJAN

DAVULE

TOUTLE

WRAITE

LABBED

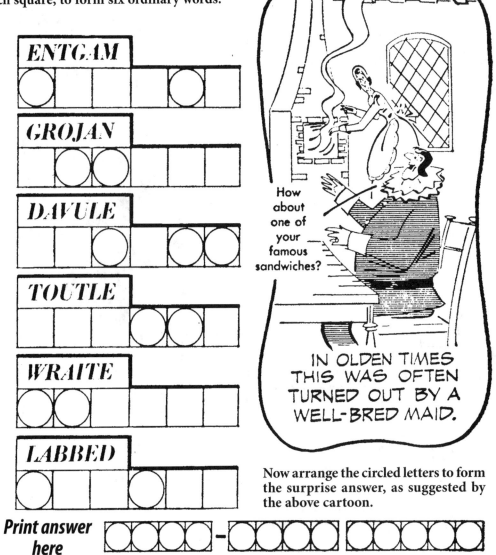

How about one of your famous sandwiches?
IN OLDEN TIMES THIS WAS OFTEN TURNED OUT BY A WELL-BRED MAID.

Now arrange the circled letters to form the surprise answer, as suggested by the above cartoon.

Print answer here

JUMBLE®

Unscramble these six Jumbles, one letter to each square, to form six ordinary words.

DEHEAB

YASQUE

FILRAY

WALCOL

ERASHE

NUCLUR

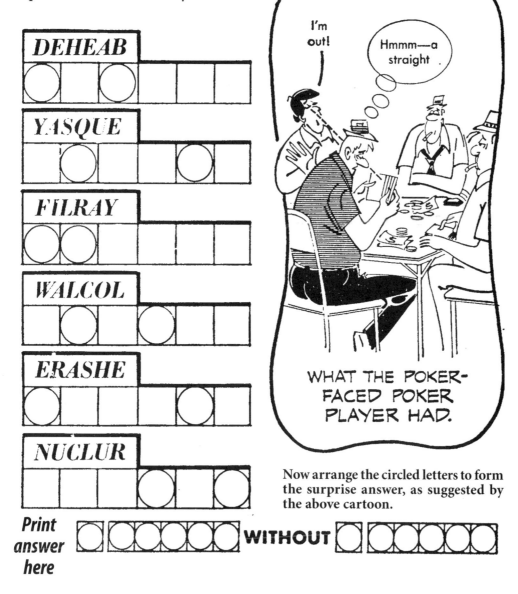

I'm out!
Hmmm—a straight
WHAT THE POKER-FACED POKER PLAYER HAD.

Now arrange the circled letters to form the surprise answer, as suggested by the above cartoon.

Print answer here ☐ ☐☐☐☐☐ WITHOUT ☐ ☐☐☐☐☐

JUMBLE®

Unscramble these six Jumbles, one letter to each square, to form six ordinary words.

TICUND

LENCAG

WOLTAL

DAVRIE

JAVILO

ROHORR

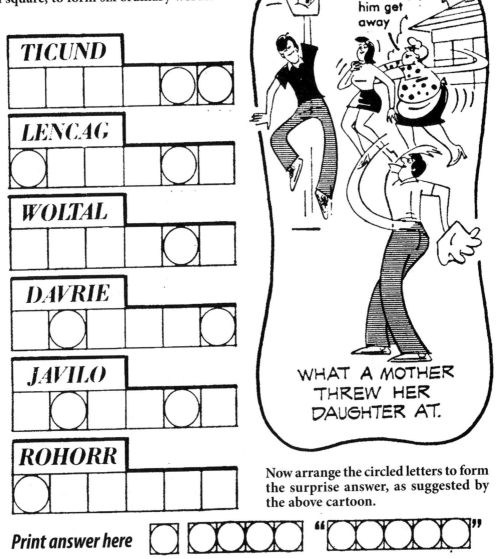

Don't let him get away
WHAT A MOTHER THREW HER DAUGHTER AT.

Now arrange the circled letters to form the surprise answer, as suggested by the above cartoon.

Print answer here _ _ _ _ _ "_ _ _ _ _ _"

PUZZLE 178

JUMBLE®

Unscramble these six Jumbles, one letter to each square, to form six ordinary words.

MALFEE

GATHIL

TYSSEM

ENBOAM

NORMED

INGALD

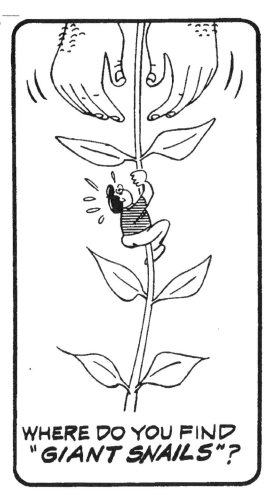

WHERE DO YOU FIND "GIANT SNAILS"?

Now arrange the circled letters to form the surprise answer, as suggested by the above cartoon.

Print answer here AT THE END OF ______' _______

PUZZLE 179

JUMBLE®

Unscramble these six Jumbles, one letter to each square, to form six ordinary words.

WHARKE

BRUZZE

DEVAUL

ALOONG

SMIFLY

GAIDOA

WHAT PALEONTOLOGY MAY BE A FORM OF.

Now arrange the circled letters to form the surprise answer, as suggested by the above cartoon.

Print answer here “ ◯◯◯◯◯ - ◯◯◯◯◯◯◯ ”

PUZZLE 180

JUMBLE®

Unscramble these six Jumbles, one letter to each square, to form six ordinary words.

GINKAB

LAPTEA

MEDOCY

TIMLEG

CREFOD

NECCAT

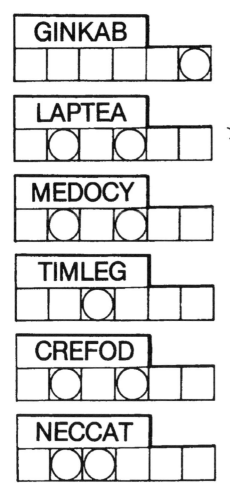

BANG!
WHAT THE ROBOT SAID WHEN THERE WAS A POWER FAILURE.

Now arrange the circled letters to form the surprise answer, as suggested by the above cartoon.

Print answer here "□. □. □□□□, □. □. □□"

ANSWERS

1. **Jumbles:** ABBEY CRANK NATURE TIMELY
Answer: Bigmouthed at the summit!—A CRATER

2. **Jumbles:** DELVE FIFTY TRIPLE INLAID
Answer: Why the results of his physical were music to his ears—HE WAS FIT AS A FIDDLE

3. **Jumbles:** PEONY GRAIN BIKINI SAVORY
Answer: Once is OK, but a repeat means prison—SING

4. **Jumbles:** MOUSY APPLY WEAKEN TUMULT
Answer: What the stupid shoplifter was—SLOW ON THE UPTAKE

5. **Jumbles:** RIVET BRAIN CENSUS FACILE
Answer: The cartoonist drew this in order to hide what he was doing—A CURTAIN

6. **Jumbles:** OCTET STEED POPLIN CAVORT
Answer: What the scared tree was—ROOTED TO THE SPOT

7. **Jumbles:** BASIS YEARN CLOVER POUNCE
Answer: Openings provided for stereo sound—YOUR EARS

8. **Jumbles:** NIPPY DAUNT SMUDGE TUXEDO
Answer: What the burlesque queen was responsible for—HER OWN "UNDOING"

9. **Jumbles:** BOUGH LATHE FRUGAL DRIVEN
Answer: This old-fashioned garment sounds like two—A DOUBLET

10. **Jumbles:** STOIC VISOR EXHALE FORGER
Answer: The kleptomaniac's favorite restaurant—THE SELF-SERVICE

11. **Jumbles:** FORUM METAL CORRAL BANGLE
Answer: What some girls do for attention—"GLAMOUR" FOR IT

12. **Jumbles:** DINER SHAKY POPLAR CASHEW
Answer: When the weather is bad, only these should take to the streets—HARDY SOLES

13. **Jumbles:** BOGUS DRONE ANKLET MYSELF
Answer: What women who know all the answers never get—ASKED

14. **Jumbles:** GRIEF TWEET DAMASK NIPPLE
Answer: How women are after shopping sprees—TIRED—AND SPENT

15. **Jumbles:** WHOOP SNORT DABBLE CURFEW
Answer: What the traffic cop turned doctor warned his patient to do—SLOW DOWN

16. **Jumbles:** MOUND AROMA TIPTOE BAFFLE
Answer: What Adam wasn't—ADAMANT

17. **Jumbles:** AFOOT GRIMY DARING HECKLE
Answer: What you have to get to wallpaper a room—THE HANG OF IT

18. **Jumbles:** ELOPE BIRCH HAUNCH GAINED
Answer: Fruit sometimes found in the sand—A BEACH PEACH

19. **Jumbles:** BROOK AGLOW NINETY IMPEND
Answer: Why you shouldn't criticize nudists—THEY WERE BORN THAT WAY

20. **Jumbles:** TOXIC SPURN DECODE YEOMAN
Answer: What to avoid if you married your wife for her looks—DIRTY ONES

21. **Jumbles:** CHAMP JUDGE BUMPER PAGODA
Answer: What the hip grocer said his "bag" was—PAPER

22. **Jumbles:** GOING VALVE POORLY FATHOM
Answer: Your wife might do this when you give—FORGIVE

23. **Jumbles:** VIPER FLORA FLURRY TROPHY
Answer: What the boss's son-in-law usually is—"FIRE" PROOF

24. **Jumbles:** BRINY CRAWL GRIMLY CRAFTY
Answer: What some women do if at first they don't succeed—CRY, CRY AGAIN

25. **Jumbles:** BILGE TYPED PALATE HAGGLE
Answer: It seems only natural that "Scotch" should make you this—"TIGHT"

26. **Jumbles:** AIDED VERVE PSYCHE CALIPH
Answer: What some of today's youth seem to prefer—VICE TO ADVICE

27. **Jumbles:** HUSKY THYME FERVID COUSIN
Answer: What the poolroom hustler turned actor never missed—THE CUE

28. **Jumbles:** KEYED IVORY TYPIST MAINLY
Answer: When a bachelor gives a girl plenty of rope, this is how he might find himself—TIED IN A KNOT

29. **Jumbles:** TAFFY INEPT FINALE DIVERT
Answer: How to get the boss to let you go home early—FEINT A FAINT

30. **Jumbles:** LEECH SOOTY RANCID CARNAL
Answer: What the long green often shows up—ONE'S REAL COLORS

31. **Jumbles:** DUMPY BATCH MEASLY NOVICE
Answer: What the old-time brewers called their annual shindigs—"HOPS"

32. **Jumbles:** AXIOM DOWNY HAZARD PIGEON
Answer: What eventually happened to the guy who stayed up all night wondering where the sun went to when it set—IT DAWNED ON HIM

33. **Jumbles:** COMET FAMED PICKET GOVERN
Answer: This might separate two quarreling thieves—A FENCE

34. **Jumbles:** AFIRE GUILT BALSAM POETRY
Answer: What you might aim for in some circles—TARGETS

35. **Jumbles:** AVAIL CHESS HALLOW MODERN
Answer: How a fish escapes from prison—HE "SCALES" THE WALL

36. **Jumbles:** CARGO EMPTY AVENUE MYSTIC
Answer: What they said about the pretty lady cabdriver—YOU "AUTO METER"

37. **Jumbles:** ABHOR NUTTY PILLAR LIQUOR
Answer: How the dentist and his manicurist wife fought—TOOTH & NAIL

38. **Jumbles:** ICING OBESE MILDEW DILUTE
Answer: What the grease monkey got after working hours—"OILED"

39. **Jumbles:** VISTA LAUGH GARBLE INDOOR
Answer: A small depression we all have to stomach—THE NAVEL

40. **Jumbles:** LIGHT BRAVE FLORAL MAGPIE
Answer: What an electrical charge means—A BILL

41. **Jumbles:** DECRY HAVEN MUSKET NOODLE
Answer: A kind of surreptitious ball playing—"UNDERHAND"

42. **Jumbles:** ANNUL FAULT BAMBOO HOMING
Answer: What the boss said when asked how many people worked in his office—ABOUT HALF

43. **Jumbles:** ICILY KNACK SHOULD MANAGE
Answer: What the manicurist wanted to do—NAIL HIM

44. **Jumbles:** POKED VISTA UNLIKE SCENIC
Answer: What he thought the restaurant was—CLOSED

45. **Jumbles:** PATCH FRUIT DIGEST TEACUP
Answer: A fighting opponent—A PACIFIST

46. **Jumbles:** ARBOR EPOCH BLUISH LEGUME
Answer: "So clear" to ANCIENT priests—"ORACLES"

47. **Jumbles:** CROWN GROOM DAWNED LIKELY
Answer: Sounds like an appropriate place for an outdoor pop concert—A ROCK GARDEN

48. **Jumbles:** UNWED BRAVO SIPHON INVADE
Answer: What the nudist demonstrators did—AIRED THEIR VIEWS

49. **Jumbles:** FILMY POPPY UNTRUE ADRIFT
Answer: How to paint a sardine—IN OIL

50. **Jumbles:** COUPE PIKER NOTIFY HELPER
Answer: How to stop that ringing in your ears—PICK UP THE PHONE

51. **Jumbles:** PATIO ARRAY SCHOOL NETHER
Answer: Why he took a hammer to bed with him—TO HIT THE HAY

52. **Jumbles:** FIORD GNOME PERSON VIOLIN
Answer: He called her "Sugar" because she was this—SO REFINED

53. **Jumbles:** QUOTA DEITY LAXITY SHERRY
Answer: What she knew how to do—"DISH IT OUT"

54. **Jumbles:** DUSKY FRAUD OPIATE PAUNCH
Answer: What the billposter did for his employer—STUCK UP FOR HIM

55. **Jumbles:** RAPID NUDGE CRAVAT MALADY
Answer: Don't butter up a man who's in this business!—MARGARINE

56. **Jumbles:** JETTY AGATE RELISH WEAPON
Answer: What one lovebird called the other—"TWEETHEART"

57. **Jumbles:** LIMIT SCOUT BEDECK DREDGE
Answer: Why you should never let grass grow under your feet—IT TICKLES

58. **Jumbles:** FAVOR GUILE CUDDLE EXODUS
Answer: How he carried his business problems home—IN HIS GRIEF CASE

59. **Jumbles:** MANGE PLAID AMPERE JACKAL
Answer: Where the usher put an overattentive theatergoer—IN HIS PLACE

60. **Jumbles:** PIOUS DOGMA ARTFUL MISUSE
Answer: What the garbageman said he was, completely!—AT HER DISPOSAL

61. **Jumbles:** DERBY MOUTH CANDID ROSARY
Answer: After a dirty game, these ballplayers were all washed up—THE SCRUB TEAM

62. **Jumbles:** RAINY PIPER BEHAVE UNHOOK
Answer: What the rich wigmaker's son was—THE HAIR HEIR

63. **Jumbles:** AORTA BUSHY MANIAC PREFER
Answer: The best way to hold your man—IN YOUR ARMS

64. **Jumbles:** BUMPY FACET NAUSEA ALPACA
Answer: The caveman's favorite sandwich—CLUB

65. **Jumbles:** BANDY PARKA VIRILE CHUBBY
Answer: What people who drink to forget should do—PAY IN ADVANCE

66. **Jumbles:** LIMBO RAVEN ADROIT STYLUS
Answer: Doesn't show up until the work is finished!—A BLISTER

67. **Jumbles:** PIVOT OFTEN FORGOT PULPIT
Answer: What the button tycoon was always doing—POPPING OFF

68. **Jumbles:** CLEFT SMOKY OCELOT HYBRID
Answer: What the ballplayer did after a late night out—"STOLE HOME"

69. **Jumbles:** LINER FINAL BLOODY JOSTLE
Answer: Why he married the birdseed heiress—SHE FILLED THE BILL

70. **Jumbles:** DIZZY ABASH GUIDED BANANA
Answer: What the lunch wagon owner named his daughter—DINAH

71. **Jumbles:** UNCLE PUTTY FLORID JABBER
Answer: What she was when he complained about her overcooked biscuits—"BURNED UP"

72. **Jumbles:** MOLDY ABIDE GUTTER VALISE
Answer: What they said to the guy who was taking a trip on a tramp steamer—"BUM VOYAGE"

73. **Jumbles:** PUPIL BRAVE MARROW ADVICE
Answer: This might grow in a junkyard—A BUMPER CROP

74. **Jumbles:** SHINY TWEAK RADIUM PAUPER
Answer: What the silver tycoon's reputation was—TARNISHED

75. **Jumbles:** ERUPT SKIMP VERSUS DIVIDE
Answer: There's a female in the middle of this type of society—"PER-MISS-IVE"

76. **Jumbles:** MAIZE SWOON BOTTLE PRAYER
Answer: What they might have at an Italian picnic—"ROME-ANTS"

77. **Jumbles:** CURVE VALET INVITE FELLOW
Answer: French toast—VIVE LA FRANCE

78. **Jumbles:** ELDER CYCLE HUNTER SYSTEM
Answer: What the wise old owl practiced—WHAT HE SCREECHED

79. **Jumbles:** SINGE GAUDY PUSHER BEAUTY
Answer: Small cars relieve this—GAS "PAYIN'S"

80. **Jumbles:** IDIOT NAVAL TAWDRY CANYON
Answer: What a thirsty man might do in Formosa—"TAIWAN" ON

81. **Jumbles:** RODEO SNARL CAMPUS PAYOFF
Answer: The wool salesman's stock-in-trade—COARSE YARNS

82. **Jumbles:** AGING CHANT NEWEST ECZEMA
Answer: Where you might find good French soup—IN "CANNES"

83. **Jumbles:** CHAIR WHEAT FACTOR DEAFEN
Answer: A shotgun wedding—WIFE OR DEATH

84. **Jumbles:** OLDER AHEAD HEREBY UNRULY
Answer: What they said when Venus of Milo came to dinner—YOU GOTTA HAND IT TO HER!

85. **Jumbles:** RAJAH SUEDE ADJUST FAULTY
Answer: What low-calorie shampoos are good for—FATHEADS

86. **Jumbles:** KINKY PARTY IMPOSE DECENT
Answer: How he got to be chief engineer—HE HAD AN INSIDE TRACK

87. **Jumbles:** DAILY VENOM CHORUS SEPTIC
Answer: What they said the lady cattle rancher had—NICE CALVES

88. **Jumbles:** MAGIC THICK ANYHOW PLEDGE
Answer: How Santa arrived—IN THE "NICK" OF TIME

89. **Jumbles:** YACHT NOISY DRUDGE FUMBLE
Answer: What a stag guest at the annual surgeons' dance said—MAY I CUT IN?

90. **Jumbles:** LINGO DRAMA PARODY ALWAYS
Answer: What a gal who took up law did after she got married—LAID IT DOWN

91. **Jumbles:** OUNCE PHOTO GIGGLE BEHELD
Answer: What you get when you cross a dog with a hen—A POOCHED EGG

92. **Jumbles:** EXCEL RURAL DEPUTY MEDLEY
Answer: Where they might put a man who's been convicted of assault...and battery—IN A DRY CELL

93. **Jumbles:** ARBOR EVENT BUTLER DONKEY
Answer: The last guy to box this fighter—THE UNDERTAKER

94. **Jumbles:** PLUME SOUSE AFRAID BELIEF
Answer: A good thing to do for insomnia—SLEEP IT OFF

95. **Jumbles:** SOGGY BROOD KIMONO SLEIGH
Answer: The artist's model only worked when this happened—HER BOSS WAS LOOKING

96. **Jumbles:** GOOSE PHONY FROSTY BOTANY
Answer: Odd if they're both right!—SHOES

97. **Jumbles:** PIVOT FORUM DENTAL MIDDAY
Answer: It's the same in many countries—"DITTO"

98. **Jumbles:** RODEO PIANO BICEPS ERMINE
Answer: Gets paid after his work is finished—A PENSIONER

99. **Jumbles:** POUND CROUP ASYLUM SIPHON
Answer: This is neither very good nor very bad—so, repeat it!—SO-SO

100. **Jumbles:** PHOTO DAILY BOTTLE FLORID
Answer: Why the gunman and his gun were dangerous—BOTH WERE LOADED

101. **Jumbles:** TEPID CHAFF BEHAVE GHETTO
Answer: What the proud giraffe kept—HER HEAD HIGH

102. **Jumbles:** OCCUR ELOPE TINKLE OFFSET
Answer: What he said he would do when his workers demanded a raise—REFLECT ON IT

103. **Jumbles:** YEARN CUBIC TROUGH UNTRUE
Answer: Seems to be a "trick" to fastening it—A "CATCH"

104. **Jumbles:** HELLO CREEK GUNNER DURESS
Answer: Poured on the politician—SCORN

105. **Jumbles:** MAIZE BRAIN SHOULD PELVIS
Answer: What the pretty tattoo artist made on her customers—AN IMPRESSION

106. **Jumbles:** ARBOR FAUNA GUILTY BLEACH
Answer: This rather uncouth character has a couple of bars—A "BAR-BAR-IAN"

107. **Jumbles:** MERGE CHICK PLENTY REDUCE
Answer: What you might like the butcher to slice—THE PRICE

108. **Jumbles:** SILKY NAVAL BEMOAN TIMING
Answer: "Am I able? Could be friendly!"—"AMIABLE"

109. **Jumbles:** PROBE ABATE HAPPEN INSIST
Answer: Could be the reason—for having married in Spain—"THE SENORA"

110. **Jumbles:** LATCH SIXTY MISHAP GIBLET
Answer: How the cops spotted the fence—BY HIS "GAIT"

111. **Jumbles:** OWING EMERY AMAZON FORBID
Answer: What you might find in Borneo—on a native—"NO ROBE"

112. **Jumbles:** KNOWN LISLE TUXEDO INJECT
Answer: What he blamed his bad luck on—A JINX AT THE LINKS

113. **Jumbles:** NIPPY MOUND GLANCE EMPIRE
Answer: What you'd expect to pay for an acupuncture treatment—PIN MONEY

114. **Jumbles:** CHAOS GIVEN FETISH SEXTON
Answer: How an angry dentist grinds teeth—HE GNASHES

115. **Jumbles:** HUMID GLOVE EXOTIC PIGEON
Answer: What "tequila" is—THE "GULP" OF MEXICO

116. **Jumbles:** FILMY ABOVE GUITAR INVOKE
Answer: What he came into when he was born—BEING

117. **Jumbles:** TASTY FLUTE WHINNY ORIGIN
Answer: The train carrying the laundrymen to work was delayed because of this—"WASH OUT" ON THE LINE

118. **Jumbles:** ADULT LINEN PONCHO INFANT
Answer: What you have to take into consideration these days when you have your tires pumped up—INFLATION

119. **Jumbles:** ABOUT FOCUS SALOON PARDON
Answer: The boss is "upset"—and bursts into tears—"SOBS"

120. **Jumbles:** HIKER SHOWY GOSPEL BOUGHT
Answer: "Historical" is the word for this Presidential address!—THE WHITE HOUSE

121. **Jumbles:** CHESS CRAFT MORBID GRAVEN
Answer: Threatened to rain on the actors at the outdoor theater—"OVER CAST"

122. **Jumbles:** AGLOW SKUNK BURLAP FACADE
Answer: Only royalty have such overhead problems—CROWNS

123. **Jumbles:** SWOOP LEGAL EMBODY AMOEBA
Answer: What he did around the house when told he was too young to have a moped—"MOPED"

124. **Jumbles:** DIRTY HEFTY JOSTLE CRABBY
Answer: Come in this and you'll win!—FIRST

125. **Jumbles:** OAKEN WHISK ARTFUL MASCOT
Answer: Agitated where cocktails are concerned—THE SHAKER

126. **Jumbles:** ANISE TWEET CARNAL INVADE
Answer: Not odd to be in the seventies!—"EVEN"

127. **Jumbles:** VOUCH BRAWL ERMINE CAVORT
Answer: A bad habit might get a "grip" on one—A "VICE"

128. **Jumbles:** UTTER STAID BICKER ENMITY
Answer: "He likes you a lot, but he could be married"—"ADMIRER"

129. **Jumbles:** JULEP PANDA ORPHAN SEPTIC
Answer: What bargain-priced cameras might be—"SNAPPED" UP

130. **Jumbles:** JEWEL TYPED OSSIFY BROKER
Answer: For those who train by night—SLEEPERS

131. **Jumbles:** LEECH INKED BEACON SALUTE
Answer: Not the first man to be involved in a duel!—THE SECOND

132. **Jumbles:** SWISH PEONY KENNEL DOOMED
Answer: The crook got chummy, then pulled a confidence trick—"HOOD-WINKED"

133. **Jumbles:** GAUGE AFOOT CANDID FORGOT
Answer: Rather old-fashioned—but managed to go out with boys nevertheless—"DATED"

134. **Jumbles:** SWAMP TROTH UNLOAD GAMBLE
Answer: Evidently they didn't sit down when they made this toast—"BOTTOMS UP"

135. **Jumbles:** FETCH LEAFY DEVICE INLAND
Answer: In the best of health despite being high-strung—FIT AS A FIDDLE

136. **Jumbles:** UNCLE TOXIC COMMON VORTEX
Answer: Could be "mad"—but with a motive—"LOCO"-MOTIVE

137. **Jumbles:** HOARY FLOUT SLOUCH EULOGY
Answer: What he was when he was finished with the drilling—"THROUGH"

138. **Jumbles:** FLUKE GNARL INTENT BELIEF
Answer: What he hoped to get from the baker—A "BREAK"

139. **Jumbles:** INLET PROXY LEGUME VARIED
Answer: "Am pleased to have enough to start with"—"AMPLE"

140. **Jumbles:** ITCHY COLIC NEARLY SIMILE
Answer: They often hang about in the cold—ICICLES

141. **Jumbles:** ELUDE GOUGE DAWNED AGENCY
Answer: What a hearty Scotsman might consider a seven-day case of the flu—JUST A WEE COLD

142. **Jumbles:** SORRY ABBEY CALMLY TEAPOT
Answer: A sound increase in business—BOOM!

143. **Jumbles:** BLIMP ACRID CEMENT HELPER
Answer: What he got when he went to one of those "high-class" hair stylists—"CLIPPED"

144. **Jumbles:** LEAKY FAMED BECAME JOVIAL
Answer: Could be claimed—to be a matter for the doctor—"MEDICAL"

145. **Jumbles:** CREEL SOGGY UNEASY GUIDED
Answer: Even better than a close friend—A GENEROUS ONE

146. **Jumbles:** UNIFY GLEAM HALVED SLUICE
Answer: How he showed impatience with his neighbors who were polluting the air—HE "FUMED"

147. **Jumbles:** GLOAT KNACK PALLID ENTAIL
Answer: Where you might sleep when you're put up for the night—THE ATTIC

148. **Jumbles:** BUSHY DRYLY AGHAST FABLED
Answer: What you would expect to find plenty of in a military band composed mainly of officers—"BRASS"

149. **Jumbles:** DIZZY EXUDE FACING BEYOND
Answer: More than an igloo—even if ice is largely used in its construction—"ED-IF-ICE"

150. **Jumbles:** MOUSY BROOK DITHER HAGGLE
Answer: What the dermatologist's behavior was, to say the least—"RASH"

151. **Jumbles:** BEGOT CAKED KIMONO HANDLE
Answer: From sergeant to corporal!—DEMOTED

152. **Jumbles:** AUGUR SYLPH LACKEY HAZARD
Answer: It requires an effort of will to leave it—A LEGACY

153. **Jumbles:** FUDGE KNAVE CHALET ENGULF
Answer: What a good make-up job is worth—
ITS FACE VALUE

154. **Jumbles:** SOLAR LOATH IMPORT GENTLE
Answer: Sounds comfortably sick—"ILL AT EASE"

155. **Jumbles:** SNOWY EXTOL PEPTIC MALADY
Answer: One paw of a big lion could be a dangerous one—WEAPON

156. **Jumbles:** NERVY JUDGE SUGARY FIASCO
Answer: When soldiers do it they usually look right—"DRESS" (dress right)

157. **Jumbles:** EXULT BRAVO UNSAID SEETHE
Answer: "You and I and no one else!"—OURSELVES

158. **Jumbles:** SAVOR TYING OCCULT FICKLE
Answer: Shrink from a business deal—"CONTRACT"

159. **Jumbles:** JINGO BELLE SUBTLY CANKER
Answer: The part of a woolen sock you can sometimes see through—"LENS"

160. **Jumbles:** SKIMP BRINY CONVEX HAUNCH
Answer: What time and grime do—RHYME

161. **Jumbles:** DETAIN ICEBOX FORAGE BARREL CLOTHE HANDLE
Answer: What he said when asked why he stole a purse—
I NEEDED THE CHANGE

162. **Jumbles:** BRANDY DAMAGE SPLICE CLOUDY INFANT SWIVEL
Answer: What he hoped the hula dancer would be—
EASILY SWAYED

163. **Jumbles:** EMPLOY CAUCUS GENDER BISECT POETIC RABBIT
Answer: Why good authors never write on an empty stomach—PAPER'S BETTER

164. **Jumbles:** ASPECT GHETTO WISDOM BELFRY POLLEN CABANA
Answer: Why the vampire avoided her—
WRONG BLOOD TYPE

165. **Jumbles:** ENCORE PETITE UPSHOT DEFAME PILFER BANNER
Answer: No matter how early the judge started work, he always found this—PEOPLE UP BEFORE HIM

166. **Jumbles:** RAGLAN ARMORY BUNION SYMBOL FILLET MEMOIR
Answer: A metronome can determine the speed with which you go—FROM BAR TO BAR

167. **Jumbles:** STOOGE DUPLEX ARCTIC REALTY INDOOR GADFLY
Answer: What the ghoul said when asked whether he had stolen the body—"OF CORPSE!"

168. **Jumbles:** GOSPEL ORIOLE HOTBED TRUANT AIRWAY BETAKE
Answer: An alarm clock can scare this—
THE DAYLIGHT INTO YOU

169. **Jumbles:** BROKER JINGLE TOWARD UNCLAD FOIBLE CANOPY
Answer: How Betsy Ross knew what the Founding Fathers wanted—SHE TOOK A FLAG "POLL"

170. **Jumbles:** SOLACE PODIUM HANGAR CORNER UPLIFT APATHY
Answer: What they called the gal who married a long-haired guy in Mississippi—MRS. HIPPIE

171. **Jumbles:** CAUGHT IMPORT ABACUS MOTHER OSSIFY SOOTHE
Answer: What the leopard said when he finished his dinner—
THAT HIT THE SPOTS

172. **Jumbles:** MANAGE HECKLE FORBID UNCURL ASSAIL BRONCO
Answer: What he got when he picked a four-leaf clover growing in the midst of all that poison ivy—
A RASH OF GOOD LUCK

173. **Jumbles:** HUNTER GIBBON COMPLY AERATE SHOULD BODICE
Answer: What someone did to the thirsty boxer—
BEAT HIM TO THE "PUNCH"

174. **Jumbles:** SPRUCE JAGGED ELICIT GUZZLE LUNACY EGOISM
Answer: Why some couples go to "court"—
TO PLAY "SINGLES"

175. **Jumbles:** MAGNET JARGON VALUED OUTLET WAITER DABBLE
Answer: In olden times this was often turned out by a well-bred maid—WELL-MADE BREAD

176. **Jumbles:** BEHEAD QUEASY FAIRLY CALLOW HEARSE UNCURL
Answer: What the poker-faced poker player had—
A FLUSH WITHOUT A BLUSH

177. **Jumbles:** INDUCT GLANCE TALLOW VARIED JOVIAL HORROR
Answer: What a mother threw her daughter at—
A GOOD "CATCH"

178. **Jumbles:** FEMALE ALIGHT SYSTEM BEMOAN MODERN LADING
Answer: Where do you find "giant snails"?—
AT THE END OF GIANTS' FINGERS

179. **Jumbles:** HAWKER BUZZER VALUED LAGOON FLIMSY ADAGIO
Answer: What paleontology may be a form of—
"SKULL-DUGGERY"

180. **Jumbles:** BAKING PALATE COMEDY GIMLET FORCED ACCENT
Answer: What the robot said when there was a power failure—"A.C. COME, A.C. GO"

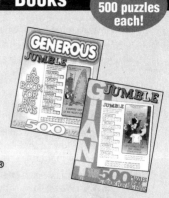

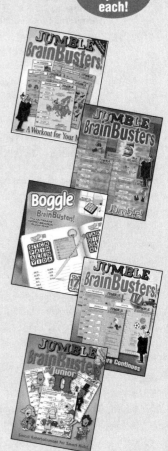